Reinvigorating IOR-ARC

Reinvigorating IOR-ARC

Edited by

Vijay Sakhuja

INDIAN COUNCIL OF WORLD AFFAIRS

INDIAN OCEAN RESEARCH GROUP

PENTAGON PRESS

Reinvigorating IOR-ARC / *Vijay Sakhuja* (Ed)

ISBN 978-81-8274-598-8

First Published in 2012

Published by
PENTAGON PRESS
206, Peacock Lane, Shahpur Jat,
New Delhi-110049
Phones: 011-64706243, 26491568
Telefax: 011-26490600
email: rajan@pentagonpress.in
website: www.pentagonpress.in

Printed at
Aegean Offset Printers, Greater Noida

Contents

Foreword

The IOR-ARC is now 14 years old ever since it was inaugurated in Mauritius in 1997. It is a unique exercise in regionalism bringing together as it does countries from three continents namely: Asia, Africa and Australia. That this Association has both developing countries, developed countries as well as emerging economies adds to its distinctiveness. This Association was also conceived with the idea that any attempt towards regional or sub-regional cooperation can progress well only if it is based on a holistic approach combining state to state as well as academic and business level interaction.

Right from the beginning, the agenda of IOR-ARC primarily centred on areas such as trade and investments, science and technology, education and training, piracy, natural disasters, communicable diseases, etc. The membership of this Association saw rapid increase from a core group of seven to the present figure of eighteen with five Dialogue Partners. The apex body of the IOR-ARC is the Council of Foreign Ministers (CoM). The Association had a charter drawn up from the very beginning which has now happily been revised at the last ministerial meeting in Yemen with a view to revitalising the Association. A tri-continental Association of this kind may not have been able to make marked progress especially with regard to a preferential trading arrangement or a free trade agreement. With such arrangements in place or being negotiated in each of the three continents and their sub-regions an IOR-ARC vide FTA may have been difficult to come about. The lack of progress in effective cooperation in the Association could perhaps be due to the complex geo-political and economic circumstances that prevailed in the IOR region in the recent years. However, the growing significance of the Indian Ocean itself today calls for cooperative approach among the littoral countries. Indeed with expanding globalisation and the growing needs for energy security, the Indian Ocean is fast becoming the key region for global security. Today major political conflicts are taking place around this region, where concerns for security against threats of terrorism are being witnessed. On the other hand, on the economic side, several countries in the Indian Ocean region are today growing at impressive rates creating major opportunities for trade and investment. More than 60 per cent of the world energy resources are transported across the sea lanes of the Indian Ocean and the choke points of the Malacca Straits and the Strait of Hormuz are strategically vital areas.

It is against this backdrop that the importance for closer regional cooperation amongst the Indian Ocean countries cannot be over-emphasised. The need, therefore, is to reinvigorate the IOR-ARC. The regionalism which has been envisaged under IOR-ARC is mutually complementary and supportive and is also non-competitive. The decisions that were taken at the last ministerial meeting of IOR-ARC would go a long way in putting this organisation on a sound footing with a clear agenda and programme of action. There are several areas which have been identified and highlighted and now the task before the grouping is to how to harmonise them and implement them. India, which will be soon assuming the chair of the IOR-ARC, will have a special responsibility and role in this direction.

This volume is a compilation of the papers presented at the conference 'Reinvigorating IOR-ARC' organised by the Indian Council of World Affairs, New Delhi and the Indian Ocean Research Group Inc. in New Delhi in May 2011. In view of the growing importance of the Indian Ocean region as also the keen interest with which developments in this part of the world are being followed, it is hoped that this body of thought shared by participants from the Indian Ocean littorals will be particularly useful for policy makers and academics to draw long term plans for the reinvigoration of the IOR-ARC.

Ambassador S.T. Devare
Director General
Indian Council of World Affairs
New Delhi

Message

By

H.E. Morteza Sarmadi
Director General
IOR-ARC
Mauritius

I would like to first of all thank Indian Council of World Affairs (ICWA) for having invited me to deliver the keynote address for this conference, which is to evaluate mechanisms and procedures by which Indian Ocean Regionalism might be enhanced in the future. May I also congratulate the Indian Council of World Affairs (ICWA) and the Indian Ocean Research Group (IORG) for organising this conference which would promote the role of academics and contribution of "think-tanks" in the programme of the IOR-ARC. It is a great pleasure for me to speak to such a distinguished audience. There could not have been more opportune time to hold this conference by ICWA as India takes over the Chair of IOR-ARC in few months from now. There is a lot of expectation from India, by various member states to unleash a new energy into this regional forum and to give it a new direction.

I am glad to know that Senior Diplomats and officials from the Ministry of External Affairs of the Republic of India are also present in the conference today. The well-researched papers and presentations being made by distinguished academics and diplomats will surely give more insight into the future course of action which IOR-ARC needs to take in coming years.

IOR-ARC as you know was launched in 1997 in Mauritius and it currently brings together 18 countries bordering on the Indian Ocean. The launch followed discussions such as the first Inter-Governmental

Meeting of the Indian Ocean Rim Initiative held in Mauritius on 31 March 1995 and the International Forum on the Indian Ocean Region, held in Perth in June that same year.

IOR-ARC is based on the principles of open regionalism for strengthening economic cooperation and particularly on Trade and Investment. This open regionalism, which is more member-friendly than other neo-liberal regional arrangements, includes components namely, (a) Trade Liberalisation, (b) Trade and Investment Facilitation, (c) Economic and Technical Cooperation, etc.

The Charter of IOR-ARC spells out the objectives of the Association to "promote the sustained growth and balanced development of the region and of the member states, and to create common ground for regional economic co-operation". Trade, foreign investment, scientific and technological exchanges, tourism, the movement of persons on a non-discriminatory basis, and the development of infrastructure and human resources, inter-alia, poverty alleviation, promotion of maritime transport and related matters, cooperation in the fields of fisheries, trade, research and management, aquaculture, education and training, energy, IT, health, protection of the environment, agriculture, and disaster management are among its objectives. As you may know, IOR-ARC activities include several on-going topical projects and work programmes under these aforementioned areas and conducted by IOR-ARC member states of shared interests, all of which under the umbrella of three separate Working Groups, namely the Working Group on Trade and Investment (WGTI), the Indian Ocean Rim Business Forum (IORBF), and the Indian Ocean Rim Academic Group (IORAG). It was emphasised that the work programme of IOR-ARC should not duplicate what is already being done in other regional fora.

The Academic Group as well as the Business Forum have jointly contributed to the IOR-ARC work programme through their studies and with their participation at 16 meetings for each group for the last thirteen years. The studies that have been done through the IOR Academic Group and the Business Forum had been presented by eminent academics in universities and research institutes in the region. They have identified from an academic plane the potential that exists for Trade and Investment development with facts and figures collected from all the

IOR-ARC member states directly or through secondary sources such as published reports and also from databases of prestigious institutions. These academic exercises do contain important food for thought.

Over the years, the Association has been striving hard to implement a series of work programmes on trade and investment related areas. The IOR-ARC has achieved few flagship projects in the fisheries and maritime related industries, as well as the promotion and transfer of Science & Technology in the region – all of which are considered effective tools for the upliftment of our member states. IOR-ARC countries have also regularly organised trade fairs, trade exhibitions to bring the awareness of the opportunities for trade and investment within the region with a representation of all the member countries. It has simultaneously also been dealing with internal issues and has brought in various procedural changes and structural readjustment to address the need of the hour to ensure the efficiency in the working of IOR-ARC. To quote a few: (a) the frequency of council meetings were increased from once in two years to a yearly meeting; the CSO were recently made bi-annual, to ensure better supervision. A mechanism is further being worked out to hold Extra Council meetings on the sidelines of UNGA meeting, (b) the Charter was reviewed to make it move forward and action-oriented, Rules of Procedures was changed, etc., (c) recommendations were made about the modalities for strengthening coordination between the three groups namely WGTI, IORAG, and IORBF, (d) efforts are on to re-strengthen the Academic Group to ensure a direct connection between the Academic studies and the Business Forum toward action by authorities concerned to assist in the implementation. It was suggested that IORAG to develop a greater Indian Ocean research environment; foster a culture of "Indian Oceanness"; focus on matters of common concern; research aimed at enabling better regional policy outcomes; develop a stronger regional policy foundation, and enhance collective regional awareness. In this regard, recently, a consensus was reached in drafting the Terms of Reference for Academic Group, which after the Council's approval will become clear guidelines relating to, *inter-alia*, attendance at meetings of the Group, to increase the efficacy of the IORAG, (e) the clustering approach was also adopted, realising the diversity of the Member States in terms of their level of economic development, different geographical locations and their belonging to different regional groupings. It enables the IOR-ARC to take the projects even when it has the support of one lead country and four other member states, and (f) the IOR-ARC Special Fund was established as a financial mechanism for supporting and complementing the funding of projects and programmes adopted by the Association, in line with the principles and objectives enshrined in the Charter.

Also, at the Secretariat, the Directors and I have devoted sufficient time and effort to brainstorm ourselves as to how to move forward the agenda adopted by the IOR-ARC and to achieve better status on project implementation. Having said this, the challenges that face the IOR-ARC are not very difficult to understand. If I can say, it is probably, the only organisation spread over such a vast geographical locations with such a diverse group of member states. There is a large degree of variation in the levels of economic development among the member states. There are various sub-regions within the Indian Ocean Rim. And, needless to say, that the expectations of these sub-regions vary from one to another. In this background, while the main focus of the IOR-ARC is on economic co-operation, which it indeed is, but till such time a common/ mutual agreeable programme in this regard is achieved – it is necessary to continue to work on the other areas of cooperation as envisioned in the reviewed IOR-ARC Charter such as tourism, energy, disaster management and protection of environment.

I am fully conscious of the fact that a lot needs to be done to fully realise the potential of IOR-ARC. It is timely to explore how IOR-ARC member states can build momentum for an agenda that will deliver practical, useful outcomes that reinforce regional cooperation. IOR-ARC, last month, had its first Meeting of the IOR-ARC Bi-Annual Committee of Senior Officials in Australia, where the member states discussed on projects and possible adjustments to IOR-ARC priorities and working methods. IOR-ARC member states decided to send a list of the key priorities areas, which the member state would be willing to work in and that they thought the Association should be working on. That procedure, it was believed would give the Association a shorter, sharper list of priorities, which will enable it to demonstrate progress. Projects and programmes would be attached to these priorities which were most highly ranked.

The IOR-ARC remains relevant as ever. Just to give a glimpse of the potential of the Indian Ocean Region, at the risk of repetition for those of you who already know, the Indian Ocean is the world's third largest Ocean. It carries half of the world's container ships, one third of the bulk cargo traffic, two-thirds of the world's oil shipments. It is a lifeline of international trade and economy. The region is woven together by trade routes and commands control of the major sea-lanes. The Indian Ocean Rim constitutes between a quarter and a third of the world's population (close to two billion) which makes it a massive market. It is rich in strategic and precious minerals, metals and other natural resources, valuable marine resources ranging from food fisheries to raw material and energy for industries. It has abundant agricultural wealth in terms of the variety and mass of arable land, and has significant human resources and technological capabilities. Many countries of the Rim are becoming globally competitive and are developing new capacities, which can be jointly harnessed through regional cooperation efforts.

In light of the above, it is important and imperative, not only for the political reasons that the IOR-ARC should succeed, but also for humanitarian reasons, as the region contains one thirds of the world human population. If IOR-ARC succeeds and grows, it will be good for the region and the world. I know that it is a long process as it took Europe more than four decades to have an effective framework for economic integration. I, therefore, sincerely believe that this can be done with the support of our member states.

Regional cooperation will always remain essentially the affairs of the actors in the region. There is the need for few actors i.e. member states to take a more leading role. These leading actors, can be from different sub-regions within the Indian Ocean Region or it could be more developed member states with bigger economies. I urge the more developed member states to take a leading role in setting up a proactive agenda before the Organisation and to pursue it tirelessly. It should be clubbed with the mechanisms to equip the less competitive Member States and market sectors to cope better with the more competitive nature of free trade that always applies in the market integration, as we move on to a higher level. I look forward to these Member States to act as a locomotive to pull along the entire organisation and its goals.

I look forward to listening to the talks of different scholars/speakers present here today. I am sure the talks will throw light on the common areas of cooperation amongst member states, the road map to pursue them, enhanced roles that member states could play in the region, etc. I am sure the talks will discuss both the problems that plague the success of the organisation as well as the possible pragmatic solution to overcome obstacles. I also request the organisers to quickly compile the deliberations of the conference and to send a copy of the same to the IOR-ARC Secretariat for the benefit of those who would lead the Secretariat from time to time.

I once again thank ICWA for inviting me for the talk, for the courtesies extended to me and making my stay comfortable.

I wish this conference successful deliberations.

Message

By

Shri Manbir Singh
Secretary (MER)
Ministry of External Affairs
New Delhi

It is a great pleasure for me to be here. I would like to thank Ambassador Devare for inviting me. I must compliment ICWA and the Indian Ocean Research Group for taking the initiative to conceive, and so thoughtfully plan and organise this international Conference on Reinvigorating Indian Ocean Rim Association for Regional Cooperation (IOR-ARC). I am delighted to see here so many distinguished scholars, experts and analysts who have experience and interest in issues connected with the Indian Ocean Region. Their participation in this conclave over the next two days, encourages me to believe that there will be a meaningful outcome with a promise of new ideas to look at new and old issues. Let me extend a very warm welcome to all participants. To those coming from outside, I wish a comfortable and enjoyable stay in Delhi.

This programme would enable us take stock of the Indian Ocean Rim Association for Regional Cooperation (IOR-ARC) and discuss its future. The event is very timely as the Government of India will host the next IOR-ARC council of ministers' meeting later this year. I expect stimulating discussion and brainstorming at this Conference with a view to generate an outline that will impart a new vigour and vitality to the Association. As the incoming Chair of the IOR-ARC, we look forward to benefit from your collective wisdom and constructive ideas.

The people that inhabit the areas which form the coastline and shores of the Indian Ocean, interacted with each other and contributed to each other's welfare through trade much before the nation states came into being. Therefore, these ties stretch across millennia. Their trade, encouraged by the seafaring skills and shouldered on the monsoon winds, brought about cultural exchanges across the vast body of water, stories of how people lived and their beliefs, their food habits, their strengths, their weaknesses, and their value systems. Over the years, we have called this interaction a civilisational relationship. While each nation has emerged with a distinct identity, the interaction has also led to some commonality and bonding.

In the concept of the IOR-ARC, we are only trying to give an impetus to this tradition and utilise and channel the impulses that have emerged to help people of the region to improve their living standards. The basic motivation remains the same, which is to see how we can come together to pool our resources to increase our welfare through trade, investment and technology transfer. How can we equip our young people and coming generations to be more productive through education and acquisition of skills. How can we promote understanding by appreciation of each other's history, culture and traditions. This, then, is the endeavour of the IOR-ARC.

In the IOR-ARC, we have member states from three different continents, at different stages of development and those that belong to different regional groupings. But the idea of the Indian Ocean uniting us was strong enough, not only to bring us together but sustain the grouping through a period when difficult economic conditions had given rise to insular inclinations. As India prepares to moor this grouping for the next two years, we would like to take up the challenge of converting this abiding interest of people of Indian Ocean, for realising their potential for betterment and for putting together their synergies and the complementaries for the common good.

The Indian Ocean, world's third-largest ocean, may well be the most important region in the coming decades as current and emerging powers competing for resources and nations along its rim face domestic and potentially destabilising challenges. As a much acclaimed new book by Robert Kaplan, which focuses on the Indian Ocean points out "the Greater Indian Ocean...may comprise a map as iconic to the new century as Europe was to the last one" and that the Indian Ocean will "demographically and strategically be a hub of the twenty-first century world".

The Indian Ocean region (IOR) is a critical economic highway of the world. IOR is contiguous to one of the major oil producing regions of the world, and apart from the energy lifelines that cross the Indian Ocean, major trade routes also pass through this region. About 40 per cent of seaborne crude oil passes through the Strait of Hormuz, 50 per cent of the world's merchant fleet passes through the Strait of Malacca, half of the world's container traffic passes through the Indian Ocean, and the rim land accounts for 70 per cent of the traffic of petroleum products for the entire world. The Indian Ocean rim is also rich in resources, ranging from fisheries to precious minerals, from agricultural wealth to valuable human technical expertise. The region represents close to two billion people, about one-third of the world's total population. The value of the intra-trade between the member states of IOR-ARC is $ 777 billion and has the potential to grow rapidly. There are also items in which the region as a whole can become self sufficient. The strategic value of the Indian Ocean Rim, therefore, is beyond doubt, as it constitutes an enormous asset to international traders, governments and fishing communities alike.

Indian Ocean is unique and different from the Atlantic and Pacific Oceans, in the sense that it is closed to the north by the Eurasian continent and that maritime communication to the outside world is mostly restricted to a small number of choke points. All marine traffic is funnelled through these very narrow passages as they present time and cost savings over other routes.

Since the opening of the Suez Canal in 1869, the main route from Indian Ocean to the Atlantic Ocean, Europe and Northern Africa is through the Gulf of Aden, the Ban-el-Mandeb, the Red Sea, the Gulf of Suez and the Suez Canal to the Mediterranean Sea. The other main door to and from the Indian Ocean is through the Strait of Malacca and Singapore which lead to the South China Sea, Pacific Ocean and Northeast Asia. Approximately 30 per cent of the world's trade and 20 per cent global oil demand transit through the Strait of Malacca and Singapore towards Japan, South Korea, China, and other Pacific Rim countries.

Maritime security environment in the Indian Ocean region at present is fragile. The region is also marked by extreme economic diversities and is subject to a variety of asymmetric security threats that are short of state-to-state conflict and yet present an equal if not greater threat to sea lanes.

Weak governance and some areas mired with instability at the IOR littorals compound the maritime security milieu. The Horn of Africa is a particularly worrying geographical area and a source of concern at a number of levels. Rampant piracy and armed-robbery at sea are manifestations of an increasingly worrisome situation. Complicating the maritime threat picture is indication of a tactical nexus between piracy and terrorism. Fragile maritime security environment in the IOR coupled with limitations of littoral nation in enforcing oceanic governance in the region critically influences the global concern for the sea lane security in the Indian Ocean.

India and the Indian Ocean are two inseparable entities. India's past, present and future are inextricably linked with the Indian Ocean. Throughout history, India has been interacting with the lands and the peoples of its littoral states through religion, culture and other means. The ocean has had a key place in our mythology, history, culture and economic life and has shaped and influenced the worldview of the people of India and contributed to the enrichment of Indian culture, trade and civilisation. In the coming years, as India's economic growth accelerates, and the country becomes increasingly interconnected with and interdependent on the outside world for its economic development and well-being, and fulfilment of essential energy and other needs, the centrality of the Indian Ocean Region in India's domestic as well as foreign policy is going to be ever more conspicuous.

Nearly 80 per cent of India's imported oil transits through the Strait of Hormuz. At current levels of consumption, the oil import dependence of India is expected to reach over 90 per cent by 2020. India is likely to be the world's single largest importer of oil by 2050. Ensuring the unhindered flow of oil through sea lanes of the Indian Ocean will be a major maritime issue for India. The presence of approximately 6 million Indian expatriates in the Gulf who remit around US$ 30 billion annually is also an important factor in India's foreign policy. Similarly, there is a large population of our expatriates in South and East Africa, Southeast Asia as well as an increasing presence in Australia.

Prevention of illegal immigration and infiltration of terrorists using sea routes, prevention of cross border activities such as smuggling and other illegal activities like fishing, mining in the Exclusive Economic Zone of India are also going to be increasingly serious issues from the overall Indian policy perspective.

As the topic of this Conference itself suggests, the IOR-ARC needs to be reinvigorated in order to realise its true potential. We as well as other members of IOR-ARC are conscious of this imperative. In fact, over the past three years a number of steps have been initiated to reform and activate the Association. A revised Charter of IOR-ARC, Rules of Procedures, Staff Regulations and Financial Regulations were adopted in August 2010. The IOR-ARC Special Fund was established in 2006; its administrative arrangements are being revised.

Three flagship projects have been launched: IOR Regional Centre for Science and Transfer of Technology in Tehran (RCSTT) was established in 2008; the Fisheries Support Unit in Muscat has also become operational and the IOR-ARC Maritime Transport Council also in Oman, is in the pipeline. Yemen also announced its plan to establish a Regional Maritime Center with the support of the International Maritime Organisation. Further, Malaysia has indicated interest in establishing an IOR-ARC Centre for Multilateral Education. An Open University in Mauritius is also proposed to be set up with Indian technical assistance; and draft Constitution of the University Mobility in the Indian Ocean Region (UMIOR), chaired by the Association of Indian Universities (AIU), is being finalised.

As one of the founders and key members of IOR-ARC, India has constantly endeavoured to promote cooperation in the Association and share our developmental experiences. We have hosted IOR-ARC pavilion at the India International Trade Fair, IOR-ARC film festival (Delhi, February 2008); special training course on small and medium enterprises and are going to host a proposed course on 'Geo-informatics for Coastal Disaster Management' in November 2011. India also hosted an IOR-ARC cultural event in Kochi in March 2010 to mark the arrival of replica of the 9th Century boat "Jewel of Muscat". We also hosted a special course for diplomats from IOR-ARC countries at the Foreign Service Institute in May/June 2010.

As we prepare to take over the Chair of the IOR-ARC for two years, we would like to assure our IOR-ARC friends and partners of India's willingness and desire to make necessary contribution in order to revitalise the Association. We are conscious of the hope and expectations of the members from the Association and from India, as the incoming chair.

We are in the process of consulting other friends to develop our cooperative agenda; We are ready to share our experience and extend cooperation to our friends in areas of interest to them.

There is vast reservoir of goodwill and cultural affinity among the members of the Association based on our age-old historical ties. There is a need for further strengthening the strong people-to-people interaction in the field of culture, education, trade, investment, business and technical cooperation. The private sector must be encouraged to take lead in forging mutually beneficial partnerships in the broad marine ecosystem including marine transportation, shipping industry, port management, and other sectors related to coastal economies. The tragic consequences of natural disasters that have devastated Japan is a grim reminder of the imperative need for IOR-ARC member countries working together to enhance their capability to deal with such eventualities. IOR-ARC countries must find ways to work together on issues such as the mitigation of natural disasters and the establishment of early warning systems; and maritime cooperation.

IOR-ARC is perhaps the most extraordinary international grouping, as I have said before, brings together countries straddling three continents thousands of miles apart, diverse and varied in their worldviews, social and religious traditions, economic priorities and potential, and polity – and yet inextricably connected together by the ocean. This diversity of interests and capabilities can easily impede substantive cooperation, but it can also make such cooperation far more rewarding. In the plurality and diversity, we in India see immense possibilities, and a source of our richness. India is keen to see that this Association makes tangible progress on its path to unlock regional potential and deliver positive outcomes.

We are committed to do our bit to energising this important organisation. And in this context, we look forward to receiving the ideas coming out of this meeting, which would be a most useful input and guide for us.

Before I conclude, let me once again thank ICWA and IORG for organising this conference and convey my best wishes to all the participants. I wish the event great success in spurring productive and fruitful discussions.

Message

By

Professor Dennis Rumley
Chairman
Indian Ocean Research Group (IORG)
Perth, Australia

On behalf of the Indian Ocean Research Group (IORG) Inc, I would like first of all to express my deep appreciation to the Indian Council of World Affairs (ICWA), and especially to Ambassador Devare and to Dr. Vijay Sakhuja and his organising committee for arranging to bring us all together here at Sapru House in New Delhi to discuss such an important issue at such an opportune time.

The need to reinvigorate the Indian Ocean Rim-Association for Regional Cooperation (IOR-ARC) has never been more urgent. Under India's leadership, and with the strong support of Australia and the other 16 member states, I have no doubt at all that such a reinvigoration can take place. However, to ensure its success requires, above all, a clear, collective and sustainable sense of vision, a stronger degree of cooperation, bureaucratic determination, political will, and, of course, resources. In particular, there is a need for senior regional diplomats to break the vicious circle of neglect and to ensure that a reinvigorated IOR-ARC becomes and remains committed to meaningful regional outcomes.

Overall, it is clear that, following the collapse of Cold War bipolarity, regionalism has become increasingly important in world politics, especially in the context of economic globalisation. Not surprisingly, since the end of the Cold War, there has been a resurgence of interest in regionalism among policy-makers, business people, academics and others. In many parts of the world, opportunities afforded by the end of the Cold War have resulted in a significant increase in regional institutionalisation. The resultant proliferation in the number of regional groupings has led to a widespread debate over the causes and effects of regionalism, the particular functions it performs, and the ingredients that are required to assure successful regional outcomes. A critical analysis of the factors which contribute to the success or the failure of regional groupings is especially pertinent in the case of IOR-ARC since it will enable the reinvigoration of what is a unique Indian Ocean brand of maritime regionalism.

As far as IOR-ARC is concerned, it is probably fair to say that no regional politician, bureaucrat, businessperson, academic, or, indeed, anyone else, would seriously argue that this regional grouping has been a resounding success. In fact, it is likely that there are few inhabitants of the Indian Ocean Region, including most Australians, who have ever even heard of the IOR-ARC acronym. In truth, therefore, after 14 years of its existence, IOR-ARC still remains a concept. Yet this is surprising, given the increasing geopolitical importance of the Indian Ocean Region. A strategic reassessment of the significance of the Indian Ocean has been ongoing both within and outside of the region. For example, the 2009 Australian Defence White Paper has stated that the Indian Ocean will possess a much greater geostrategic significance over the next 20 years and will become much more important in Australian maritime strategy and defence planning. In his recent book, Monsoon: The Indian Ocean and the Future of American Power (2010), Robert Kaplan has also stressed the significance of the Indian Ocean to the future maintenance of US power. In this changing geo-strategic environment, the challenges facing IOR-ARC are considerable, and India's leadership role in its reinvigoration will be crucial. In order for a comprehensive reform process to be properly implemented, a number of key questions need to be confronted, including (a) What is regionalism? What are its benefits? How do we go about constructing a successful regionalism?, (b) How successful has IOR-ARC been from the perspective of member states and dialogue partners?, (c) What is/what should be the main purpose of IOR-ARC?, (d) Should the agenda of IOR-ARC become much broader?, (e) If the agenda is to broaden, then which issues are to be "off limits" and which topics are to be "on limits"?, (f) What of IOR-ARC membership? What role should the dialogue partners take?

Should both change and how? (g) What function should the three second track groups (that is, business, tourism and academic) perform? How can these groups be strengthened?, and (h) What about the organisational structure of IOR-ARC? For example, should the nature and role of the Secretariat be enhanced and how?

I am sure that we all look forward very much indeed to considering these and many other important questions over the next two days. Once again, I congratulate ICWA for taking on this timely challenge and eagerly await the deliberations.

The Contributors

Christian Bouchard is Associate Professor at the Department of Environmental Studies, Laurentian University, (Sudbury, Canada).

Dennis Rumley is the Inaugural Professor of Indian Ocean Studies, University of Western Australia. He is also the Australian Representative, Indian Ocean Rim Academic Group (IORAG) of IOR-ARC and Chairperson, Indian Ocean Research Group Inc.

Ferdi Syamsir Ishak is Director, Indian Ocean Studies Centre at Andalas University, Indonesia.

D. Ravichandran Moorthy is Senior Lecturer in School of History, Politics and Strategic Studies at National University, Malaysia.

Ruchita Beri is Senior Research Associate at Institute of Defence and Strategic Analyses, New Delhi, India.

Saman Kelegama is Director, Institute of Policy Studies, Sri Lanka.

Sanjay Chaturvedi is Professor of Political Science at Panjab University, Chandigarh, India and Vice-Chairman, Indian Ocean Research Group. He is also a Senior Visiting Research Fellow, Institute of Southeast Asian Studies (ISEAS), Singapore and Fellow, India China Institute (ICI), The New School, New York.

Timothy Doyle is Head, Centre for International Studies, Politics and Philosophy, Keele University. He is also Chair, Politics and International Studies, School of History and Politics, University of Adelaide, Australia.

Uttara Sahasrabuddhe is Associate Professor, Department of Civics and Politics, University of Mumbai, India.

William Crumplin is Associate Professor at the Department of Environmental Studies, Laurentian University (Sudbury, Canada).

Introduction

In the Indian Ocean Region, there exist several examples of important sub-regionalisms such as the BIMSTEC, Gulf Cooperation Council (GCC) and SAARC, however, there is only one region-wide grouping, i.e. the Indian Ocean Rim Association for Regional Cooperation or IOR-ARC. The IOR-ARC was created in 1997 primarily for reasons of economic cooperation. Over the years, the organisation has grown in membership, but it has had limited success due to a number of intuitional and structural limitations. Further, as some commentators have argued, successful economic regionalism often follows rather than precedes strong internal economic interaction among member states. However, there are positive indications that IOR-ARC may take on a renewed salience in the coming years due to renewed regional interest; it is likely that Indian Ocean linkages will improve in the future, not just in matters of trade, but also on a number of issues including non-traditional security threats and challenges such as sea piracy, climate change, food security, human security and environmental issues. It is also hoped that after India assumes the Chair and Australia assumes the Vice-Chair in 2011, the IOR-ARC could be invigorated and Indian Ocean regionalism strengthened and newer vistas for cooperation can be explored.

This volume is an outcome of a conference hosted jointly by the Indian Council of World Affairs (ICWA), New Delhi and the Indian Ocean Research Group (IORG), a social science policy oriented network focusing on Indian Ocean issues. The principal aim of the conference was to assess the relative successes and failures of Indian Ocean regionalism and to evaluate mechanisms and procedures by which it might be enhanced in the future. The conference examined a number of issues including the theory and practice of regionalism, and types of regionalism such as economic, security, environmental. The highlight of the conference was the regional perspectives on IOR –ARC which were shared by participants from East African and Indian Ocean States, Iran and GCC, South Asia and Southeast Asia and Australia.

The volume contains nine chapters and these address a number of issues relating to IOR-ARC.

Timothy Doyle in Chapter 1 emphasises that 'Region' and Regionalism' have emerged as important and alternative geo-political ordering principles for national and non-state actors. Doyle critically analyses (re)emergent and contested regionalisms in this area of global geo-strategic political concern and analysis as to how various notions of regionalism can be used to facilitate the process of 'building' an Indian Ocean region.

In Chapter 2, Uttara Sahasrabuddhe argues that theories have sought to analyse regionalism in different ways. The range of theories from neo-functionalist to new regionalism provide comparative perspective on success and failures of regionalisms. This is assessed on the basis of structure and attainment of objectives and ideas and norms of regionalism. The paper argues in favour of using objectives and ideas as basis of evaluating success of regionalism.

In Chapter 3 Christian Bouchard and William Crumplin offer an islands' perspective of regionalism and argue that regional integration emanate from the needs and will of neighbouring states to develop cooperation at different geographical scales, including the scale of the Indian Ocean Region.

In Chapter 4 Ruchita Beri argues that South Africa had played a crucial role in the formation of IOR-ARC, but its interest in recent times is declining due to the emergence of a number of regional and trans-regional groupings such as the African Union, IBSA and BRICS is another cause for its lesser interest in the IOR-ARC.

In Chapter 5 Saman Kelegama evaluates the IOR-ARC and notes that the grouping has not made significant progress and its operational framework of open regionalism is flawed. Also, the group lacks political leadership and vision. In order for the IOR-ARC to survive, preferential trade agreement is the solution; but this proposition is opposed to by many member states and even if the group is dissolved, members have little to lose.

In Chapter 6 Dennis Rumley notes that Australia's orientation in IOR-ARC is short lived, because its geo-political imperatives have tended to overlook Indian Ocean region. Australia has mutual dependency with Asia-Pacific, Europe and the US, as a reason it has weaker ties with Indian Ocean region. IOR is of lesser priority to Australia. However, recent geo-political developments and renewed interest in Indian Ocean regionalism have called for relooking at its 'Look West' policy.

D. Ravichandran Moorthy in Chapter 7 discusses Malaysia's interests in Indian Ocean region owing to historical trade relations with countries in this region and some cultural similarity. It has firm interest in developing bilateral cooperation with countries in this region. The main objective of the chapter is to examine Malaysia's strategic and security involvement in the Indian Ocean. The chapter is divided into three sections; the first section outlines Malaysia's historical engagement with the Indian Ocean countries, especially India and Pakistan. The second section deals with Malaysia's geo-political and security calculations with regard to the Indian Ocean, and the third section deals with the question how these calculations coupled with the recent economic factors influence Malaysia's interests in the Indian Ocean affairs.

Sanjay Chaturvedi's central argument in Chapter 8 is that the unfolding dynamics and dilemmas of climate change in the Bay of Bengal (home to the Sunderbans, one of the world's largest contiguous block of mangrove forests, shared by India and Bangladesh), epitomise and illustrate the urgency of rescaling Indian Ocean 'regionalism' and 'regional cooperation'. It looks at potential of IOR-ARC in mitigating impact of climate change and how in turn climate change could affect objectives of IOR-ARC. It is suggested that a new and nuanced social construction of the Indian Ocean space as an 'inter-regional arena' is needed for realising ecologically sustainable, socially just and equitable development of the region.

In Chapter 9, Ferdi Syamsir Ishak presents an Indonesian Perspective of the IOR-ARC. Ferdi suggests that his country sees several benefits by cooperating with Indian Ocean states. Indonesia aspires for a prominent role in the IOR-ARC and thus remains committed to strengthening the IOR-ARC.

Chapter 1

Building Indian Ocean Regionalisms: An Agenda for IORG Research

Timothy Doyle

> *'Australia must look west, to the great challenges and opportunities that now present themselves across the Indian Ocean region..., home to more than 2.6 billion people, almost 40 per cent of the world's population'.*[1]

Introduction

In global terms, the Indian Ocean (IO) has traditionally been the neglected Ocean, seen as marginal to global centres of power and conflict.[2] The IO has been rightly described as the 'Heart of the Third World' or the 'Ocean of the South', with low per capita income and low levels of development in the majority of countries. The overwhelming mass of these peoples struggle to survive under the conditions characterised by chronic poverty, precarious political systems, stagnating and struggling economies, and fragmented political systems guided by the considerations of ethnic and religious identities.[3]

From this situation of relative neglect, however, the Twenty-First Century has seen a global upsurge in interest in the IOR on the part of policy-makers, business people and academics, associated in part with a growing realisation of its enhanced geo-strategic significance. Several events have placed new emphasis on the IO environment in its broadest sense, and especially on the secure and sustainable use and management of that environment: the end of the Cold War; increasing globalisation;

India's opening up and Look East policy; the end of apartheid in South Africa; Australia's above-mentioned Look West policy; and the burgeoning concern over an array of non-traditional security threats, especially in relation to energy security.[4]

Regionalism has, since the collapse of Cold War bipolarity, become an increasingly important concept in world politics – especially in the context of economic globalisation. The post-Cold War era has witnessed, unsurprisingly, a resurgence of interest in the nature and functions of regionalism among policy-makers, business people and academics. In many parts of the world, opportunities afforded by the end of the Cold War have resulted in a significant increase in regional institutionalisation – the European Union (EU) and ASEAN, for example, have become some of the most powerful actors in the international political arena. The nature and function of regionalism in the IOR has been the subject of much debate but lends itself to deeper and more critical analysis.[5]

Much of these more recent writings on regionalisms and regionalisation refer to *new regionalism.* Hurrell writes: there are four other important characteristics of the 'new regionalism'. First, there is the emergence of 'North/South regionalism', most powerfully illustrated by NAFTA, but relevant to developments in both Europe and Asia. Second, there is the very wide variation in the level of institutionalisation, with many regional groupings consciously avoiding the institutional and bureaucratic structures of traditional international organisations and of the regionalist model represented by the EU. A third feature of the new regionalism is its multidimensional character. The dividing line between economic and political regionalism becomes ever harder to draw as the new regionalism is fed both by the end of the Cold War and the decentralisation or regionalisation of security concerns, and by developments in the global economy. Finally, and forming part of a broader resurgence of questions of identity and belonging, many parts of the world have seen a marked increase in regional awareness or regional consciousness, even if this is not always easily or unproblematically translated into concrete schemes for regional cooperation.[6]

This chapter attempts to construct a research agenda (herein called *the project*) for IORG social scientists at this early stage of constructing and 'imagining' various and *newer* and different forms of Indian Ocean

Regionalisms which will form *from* the region, rather than from a model formed in Europe, or as just a result of the end of a bi-polar world. The Indian Ocean Research Group is already imbedded in the region. In many ways, it has been involved in a form of regional academic diplomacy for over a decade, often building policy networks between countries when national governments were not dealing with each other. For example, the IORG was able to initiate discussion in Tehran on nuclear power, when this subject had become taboo in many national circles. Having built numerous symposia, networks and policy-oriented projects over the past decade in many parts of the IO, it has become increasingly obvious to the project team that it is the languages and discourses of non-traditional securities which appear, time and again, to be the opportune sites of regional bridge-building – between both state and non-state actors. This ability to discuss these trans-border issues may, in part, be a result of the essential make-up of environmental issues: they bypass the maps constructed by human politics, and demand more regional responses and challenges. In addition, of course, non-traditional security issues have traditionally been seen as the exercise of 'soft power' and, as such, not threatening the realpolitik of nation-states.

Such human and environmental security issues, including fisheries, piracy, food, water, energy, migration, climate and others, have become the political currency with which to forge more cooperative visions and policies for the region. Even in discussions within traditional security networks such as naval and other defence force symposia, for example, it is the language of human and environmental security which seems paramount. This project seeks to explore the substance of these discourses; to understand how and why, in terms of policy practice, non-traditional security issues provide the bases for shared identities and regional understandings.

This research agenda is also based on a more innovative concept of non-traditional security, one which is more inclusive of the interests of the majority of people in the IO states. By moving away from 'viewing environmental stress as an additional threat within the (traditional) conflictual, statist framework',[7] this project envisions human and environmental problem-solving as a lynchpin of cooperative models of regional security and prosperity: a region which has the potential to provide secure access to individual citizens of all countries in the IOR to basic nutrition; adequate access to healthy environments; appropriate shelter; and the security to practice a diverse range of livelihoods which are culturally and ecologically determined.[8]

Understanding Regionalisms

There exists only one truly 'all-of-government' IOR-wide governance grouping, created in 1997 primarily for reasons of economic cooperation – the Indian Ocean Rim Association for Regional Cooperation (IOR-ARC). Any serious critical evaluation of IOR-ARC will reveal that it has had limited success, due, among other things, to its restrictive scope, membership and commitment on the part of member states. Furthermore, successful economic regionalism often follows rather than precedes strong internal economic interaction among member states.[9] Nonetheless, there are indications that IO regionalism will take on a renewed salience, partly as a result of a potentially positive Australian government response to an important recent regional report,[10] but more especially when India assumes the Chair of IOR-ARC in 2011. The major part of this research project focuses on the operations of IOR-ARC.

Although much work has been done on regions elsewhere, rarely have these theoretical and jurisdictional models been applied to an IO context. The research project will address this theme in the international legal and geopolitical context provided by littoral state claims to maritime jurisdiction, which premise the fundamental, yet evolving, spatial frameworks for oceans governance in the Indian Ocean. Regions, however, are not just collections of nation-states – they also reflect different constellations of domestic interests and institutions within states. In this vein, our innovative theorisation of regions and regionalisms (what we call spatially-based 'regulatory regionalism') challenges traditional and exclusively nation-state based conceptions of regions. Changes in the scales of governance reflect the changed circumstances of new interests. For example, regional networks exist in contesting bureaucratic agencies, communities, academies and NGO sectors, and they often pre-date and inform the more formal state-centric attempts to construct regions. In this vein, the concept of regionalism has too long been captured by a certain methodological nationalism.[11]

Indeed, it is this focus on non-state actors which first led me to the substance of regionalisation. This research project is, in many ways, evidence of the confluence of two strands of research which I have been pursuing over the past decade. Obviously, as evidenced elsewhere, the work for the Indian Ocean Research Group has been paramount to pursuing this work on the politics and international relations of littoral and non-littoral states of the IO. As Co-ordinator of Human and Environmental Security for the IORG, it is obvious that my interests into non-traditional security issues are high on my own research agenda. Much of my current work engages in the broad areas of the politics and international relations of the environment. But it is one specific (some would say unlikely) research project on transnational environmental, non-governmental public sector organisations, which initially sparked my specific intellectual interests in regionalisms, and which has provided the grounding for my future methodological approach. From 2006 to 2008, with, Brian Doherty (Keele University), we worked on a large research project funded by the United Kingdom's Economic and Social Research Council, entitled 'Friends of the Earth International: Negotiating a North-South Identity'.

The Friends of the Earth International (FoEI) is a 70 country federation of national environmental groups, each of which has equal power within the organisation. FoEI is the most significant case where environmental groups from a large number of Northern and Southern countries work together on an equal basis. However, sceptics would want to know whether equal relationships are possible in practice or whether groups from the wealthier Northern countries end up dominating decision-making. Interestingly, the project produced a very rich set of quantitative and qualitative data, which I cannot do full justice to here, but we examined the questionnaire data using a variety of dependent variables, including language, age of organisation, and organisational wealth. By far the most significant factors in informing agendas, operational styles and networks, however, were (contrary to our tentative initial hypotheses) not North-South-based, but informed by regions. When FoEI faced internal divisions after 2002, the process of examining the network's identity led to a strengthening of regional structures. This was partly to counter-balance the strength of the European region, which had been in existence since 1985. It also had a participatory rationale, to increase the number of occasions when groups could meet in addition to general meetings. There are now four recognised regions: Africa, Asia-Pacific, Latin American and the Caribbean (ATALC), and Europe.

Regionalisation has had the unintended consequence of strengthening internal divisions as regions have developed distinct political identities. The Latin Americans mostly advocate anti-neoliberal and post-development politics, and the Europeans are mostly more reformist. An illustration of this is the different interpretations of the merger of three previous campaign areas of trade, corporates and international financial institutions into a new programme. The Europeans wanted this to be called Economic Justice, the Latin Americans wanted it to be called Resisting Neoliberalism and so it is known as Economic Justice – Resisting Neoliberalism (EJRN). Asia-Pacific groups tended not to use the term at all, which puzzled us as groups from this region had originally proposed it. Most AP groups preferred to use the language of community rights rather than the more ideologically specific terms 'economic justice' or 'resisting neoliberalism'.

Using regionalisms as a methodological category, we were able to observe this along with other fascinating ideological and operational debates within FoEI about the meanings of, for example, democracy, justice and environmental transformation. Also, regional networks (and an emerging pan-regional identity) became far more instrumental to the everyday politics and operations of the organisation (both in the central secretariat and in national offices), than did North-South polarities. Interestingly, in 2009, the concept of a new region, spanning the AP and the African regions was muted by key actors within the federation. The idea of an Indian Ocean Region, in this vein, is in its infancy within this transnational NGO, now dealing in emergent regional and geopolitical blocs, rather than exclusively using North-South rhetoric as an ordering and differentiating principle.

In an influential work, Sasseen has highlighted the importance of this 'denationalisation' of public governance, that is, the process through which authority and political rule increasingly spills out of national territorial containers.[12] In other words, the processes of globalisation and market reform lead not merely to the simple zero sum transfer of power from nation-states to international liberal institutions (or NGOs), but also to a *reconstitution of the scales* upon which governance takes place. We use the notion of 'scale' in this project to exemplify the way in which political and economic actors organise, construct, and mobilise their activities and political projects around a political geographic scale of governance – for example, the local, national, regional or global.[13] Rather than seeing regionalism as the *dissolution* of the state, we argue that it may be better to think in terms of a *re-territorialisation* of the state. Here, the geophysical is reprioritised.

Constructing a Research Agenda

Our spatial approach to regionalism leads us to wrestle with the changing organisation, meaning and function of state territorial borders. The research project asks: why have these notions of regionalisms become salient at this time? What kinds of political coalitions are driving these different notions of regionalism, and what are their predominant concerns? What are the geopolitical imaginations which create and define the IOR? How are these divergent ideas crystallised into specific political programmes of action, processes and policy instruments? How are these new spaces of regional governance organised? And what interests are privileged within them? These multiple regionalisms are underpinned by a range of different interests, discourses, and institutional frameworks. Regionalism is a political project not only of state, but also non-state actors, and our approach is distinctive in taking these political projects seriously. It is not the formality or informality of the region which is significant here, but the way in which new spaces of governance are created through various regional projects.

Preliminary research and experience by the IORG Project Team to date suggests that regionalism in general, and the IOR in particular, will rapidly take on increasing geopolitical importance – but also that such notions and apparatuses of regionalism are evolving from both within the state and at the sub-state, sub-regional levels. The specified aims of this research project, then, have been designed to address both empirical and theoretical gaps in existing knowledge relating to (a) what is the level of regional integration in the IOR; (b) how can it be further developed; and (c) what are the issues and opportunities for governments and the broader region's peoples emerging from these processes. In this, we have constructed an over-arching aim i.e. to document current attempts at building pan and sub-regional identities and institutions across the Indian Ocean region, and to assess the capacity of various notions of regionalism to facilitate the process of 'building' an Indian Ocean region. The five objectives of the project, which derive from the overarching aim are:

(1) To critically assess the maritime jurisdictional claims and approaches of the Indian Ocean states with a view to assessing the emergence of a regional approach to oceans governance and to highlight convergence and divergence from international and regional norms with respect to the law of the sea;
(2) To provide an in-depth analysis of the operational governance (past, present and future) of the largest and most ambitious attempt at pan-regional governance in the Indian Ocean, the Indian Ocean Rim Association for Regional Cooperation (IOR-ARC);
(3) Using a spatially-informed theoretical approach we describe as 'regulatory regionalism', to produce a study of two very different additional regional bodies, constructing very different pan-regionalisms: the Indian Ocean Tuna Commission (IOTC) and the Indian Ocean Naval Symposium (IONS);
(4) To investigate the currency and uses of non-traditional security arguments and policy-making, as a means of building bridges, creating regional dialogues, and constructing shared regionalisms;
(5) To provide a directory of all sub-regional bodies operating in the IOR, and to conduct an extensive network analysis, describing interrelationships, shared and divergent identities and geopolitical aspirations between these bodies and other pan-regional bodies, state actors, sub-state actors, corporations, and non-state actors.

Objective 1 will enable us to understand the formal and informal structures of maritime jurisdiction, map-making and policy-making. We will assess the regional approach of the Indian Ocean littoral states to the key overarching international legal framework governing claims to maritime space, the 1982 United Nations Convention on the Law of the Sea (LOSC) (United Nations, 1983). In accordance with LOSC the spatial extent of the maritime claims of the Indian Ocean coastal states has increased dramatically (especially with the introduction of 200 nautical mile breadth exclusive economic zones (EEZ). Most Indian Ocean states have become parties to LOSC, their maritime claims are largely in keeping with its terms as far as their spatial extent is concerned, and this represents a unifying backdrop to regional oceans governance. However, LOSC offers considerable scope for differing interpretations of key provisions such as those concerning baselines, marine scientific research, navigational rights and the conduct of military operations within EEZs. This part of the project will provide an important jurisdictional spatial context for the remainder of the project and seek to assess convergences and divergences from international and regional norms of interpretation of LOSC with a view to discerning the emergence of a distinctly regional approach. It is important to realise that the maritime jurisdictional claims and rights of the Indian Ocean states are still evolving. For example, as recently as 2009, 13 Indian Ocean states asserted jurisdiction over seabed areas seawards of their 200 nautical mile limits (so-called 'extended' or 'outer' continental shelf areas). These represent a major addition to the maritime jurisdiction of these states as well as adding significant additional complexity to the maritime jurisdictional picture in the Indian Ocean region as multiple 'new' maritime boundaries have been created as a result. Largely, because of their recent vintage, these claims have yet to be subject to significant critical evaluation, but will be covered in this part of the project. We will employ a 'geolegal' research approach to the analysis of maritime jurisdictional and law of the sea issues in the IOR, reflecting IORG's multidisciplinary expertise. This involves the collection and analysis of relevant international law and policy instruments and legislation allied to geotechnical analysis using specialised geographical information systems (GIS) software coupled with satellite imagery, aerial photography and digital charting.

Objectives 2 and 3 will reveal the differing notions of regulatory regionalism that inform the three most currently visible pan-regional organisations in the IOR: the IOR-ARC, the IOTC, and the IONS. Objective 2 of the research project – an analysis of IOR-ARC – will be centred upon a detailed questionnaire and interview schedule, to be carried out across the organisation. The Indian Ocean Research Group (IORG) was granted observer status of the IOR-ARC in 2010, and will therefore attend annual meetings over the three year period. At the first meeting an initial questionnaire will be distributed, and at subsequent meetings in-depth interviews will be held with regional representatives. In addition, archives will be accessed detailing the mechanics of decision-making and governance within the body. IOR-ARC's structural form makes it ideal for the researchers' purposes – it is sufficiently institutionalised to provide useful and legitimate parameters, as well as offering a rich archive of minutes, notes and correspondence. In this vein, therefore, it provides a large but manageable case study, making it realistically possible to examine the tensions, interactions and new alliances emerging across the IOR. Whereas, for completion of objective 3 – an analysis of the IOTC and the IONS – a similar process of questionnaires followed by in-depth interviews will be pursued. The organisations have been selected because they represent the two most active 'single-issue' pan-regional organisations working in the IOR.

Objective 4 will enable us to pursue the increasingly salient debates on non-traditional security issues and policy, through assessing the capacity of such issues to create regional dialogues and to assist in 'building' an Indian Ocean region. This part of the research project on non-traditional security issues will be based on information gleaned from all other parts of the project. Interviews and questionnaires carried out for Parts 2, 3 and 5 will include specific questions on the *types* of issues which are utilised to inform various regionalisms. We will investigate the currency and uses of non-traditional security arguments and policies as a means of creating regional dialogues and constructing shared regionalisms. This component of the project will involve an exploration of the varieties of ways in which regionalisms are articulated within IOR (in IOR-ARC, IOTC, IONS, and sub-regional groupings) with reference to non-traditional security issues such as fisheries, climate, energy, food, piracy, migration, maritime etc.

Objective 5, finally, will result in the development of invaluable policy outcomes and research tools in the form of a detailed directory of all sub-regional bodies operating in the IOR, including the nature and substance of intra and inter-relationships between these bodies and others. It is hoped that, by the conclusion of the project, we will not only have established a thorough documentation of current attempts at building pan and sub-regional identities and institutions across the IOR, but will also have developed a sophisticated understanding of how various notions of regionalism can be used to facilitate the process of 'building' an Indian Ocean Region. Our method of combining network analysis with identities and stories is central to carrying out this part of the project – mapping sub-regional groupings and their regional inter-relationships. As such, it will be carried out in two phases. In phase 1, a directory of all sub-regional bodies operating in the IOR (their objectives, operations and membership) will first be developed using publicly available information. There are an abundance of sub-regional bodies working in the IOR and phase 1 will be an ambitious undertaking; however, it is considered that the thorough identification and network analysis of all sub-regional IO organisations is essential to the accuracy of the overall project outcomes. In phase 2, a network analysis will then be developed describing intra and inter-relationships between such bodies and pan-regional bodies, state actors, sub-state actors, corporations, and non-state actors (including NGOs and academic networks). Although questionnaires will be distributed to all identified sub-regional groups, in the interest of cost-efficiencies, in-depth interviews will also be conducted. The research programme will have substantial national and regional significance in that it will enable us to understand the economic and political dynamics that contribute to the supply of public goods vital to the well-being, stability, and prosperity of countries in the IOR.

The IOR-ARC (which is certainly the most obvious and visible organisation, and remains paramount to this study) is not the only attempt at constructing regional forms of governance. Other bodies have also formed at the pan-regional level (though not at the 'all of government' level). The Indian Ocean Tuna Commission (IOTC) and the Indian Ocean Naval Symposium (IONS) are two such pan-regional bodies, each with their own distinct agencies operating within and beyond nation-states, and each arguing very different regulatory and political projects for the IOR. The Indian Ocean Tuna Commission, established in 1993 under the auspices of the UN's Food and Agriculture Organisation, is charged with managing tuna and tuna-like species within the waters of the IO and encouraging the conservation and sustainable development of the region's tuna fisheries. The organisation conducts a large number of programmes including fish tagging and data gathering, and has a current membership of 28 states, including both IO Islands, littoral states, and countries whose fleets fish in the IO. The Indian Ocean Naval Symposium, instituted in 2008, offers a template for a naval version of a pan-regional organisation, which could also be replicated for land, air and police forces. Membership is open to all regional Chiefs of Navy and has attracted a great deal of interest both within and outside of the region – the greatest threat to its continuing success is the possibility that, as it was inaugurated by India, it could be perceived as being dominated by New Delhi.

The IOTC uses the paradigm of fisheries management and the language of sustainable development; whilst the IONS uses the rhetoric of regional securitisation and naval power. Interestingly, both regional bodies have recently entered dialogues with one another, using a shared non-traditional language of environmental security and food sovereignty.[14] This leads us to another aforementioned dimension of the project: in specific terms, we will be investigating the rapid emergence of non-traditional security issues as a form of policy domain or territory, where new forms of regionalisms are contested.

Finally, sub-regional groupings are increasingly active players in the IOR. These sub-regional groupings are, in many ways, the entry point for region-oriented discussions for NGOs and community-based groups and businesses. On specific occasions, they are also the entry point for sub-national forms of governance (i.e. provincial governments) which are dealing directly with the region by either bypassing or working in partnership with their own nation-states. Some examples of the plethora of subregional groupings include: BIMSTEC (Bay of Bengal Initiative for Multi Sectoral Technical and Economic Cooperation); ReCAAP (Regional Cooperation Agreement on Combating Piracy and Armed Robbery against Ships in Asia); the GCC (Gulf Cooperation Council); and the African Union. Additionally, there have been significant and novel recent developments in terms of sub-regional and international maritime security cooperation in the context of counter-piracy operations off the Horn of Africa that have largely not been subject to critical analysis. In the interests of regional stability, it is essential to grasp the gamut and scope of these organisations' operations, and to assess their role and significance as regional political actors, as well as to comprehend their diverse, and sometimes divergent objectives and practices.

Conclusions

In addition to its significance at the geostrategic level, the project is also innovative in a theoretical light, challenging these more traditional notions of regionalism. In addition, regionalism in earlier literature has often been taken to be synonymous with *economic* regionalism. Much of the early regionalism debate, in particular, is predicated on the belief that the economic dimension of regionalism is pre-eminent.[15] This research project questions, additionally, a range of tightly-held assumptions with regard to the 'national' scope of authority, rule, and citizenship, which underpin most approaches to constructing regions.[16] This mobilisation of the politics of scale refers to the shifts and transformations of the geographies of scale occurring within the process of regulatory regionalism, as a product of myriad structural pressures and imperatives that operate 'behind the back' of political and economic actors. This is in addition to those pressures stemming from the intentional strategic choices of political and economic actors to shift their activities to new levels and forms of governance more conducive to a particular set of their interests.[17] In a related vein, it is argued that shifting scales of governance strategies 'can be understood as mediations of fundamental contradictions of spatial accumulation... [and] as means for shifting the balance within these tensions by using scaled institutions and economic processes'.[18] In this view, regional regulatory projects involve a social production of scale that seeks to legitimise a particular political economy.[19] Far from accepting assumptions of the 'national' scope of regionalism which underpin most approaches to regionalism in previous literature, this project is innovative in its alternative emphasis on the politics of scale – lending it the capacity to provide a far more sophisticated and multidimensional understanding of how regionalisms are constructed.

One of the intriguing aspects of regulatory regionalism is the way it brings into play a multiplicity of scales of governance within the state, creating novel forms of political conflict between contending regulatory regimes, which result in the less than uniform spread of regulatory projects (see IONS versus IOTC). The emerging patterns of contestation and resistance are one of the distinctive aspects of regulatory regionalism. Adopting this regulatory perspective, we argue that regional governance is not just an agglomeration of national territorial and political units at a higher regional level (creating a form of liberal institutionalism). Rather, it is a far more fundamental regionalisation which emerges at all levels of domestic, sub-regional and pan-regional governance 'spaces'.

In contrast to much of the literature on new regionalism that examines the dynamics and forms of market integration, then, our regulatory regionalism approach emphasises the constitution of broad regional regulatory projects within the institutional spaces of the state. The perspective adopted in this project highlights the way in which regional governance is focused on the *implementation and contestation* over various regulatory projects in the governance of the IOR. Central to the processes of regulatory regionalism are the new institutional structures and instruments – through which domestic regulatory agencies develop connections with both their foreign counterparts and with regional regulatory bodies, thereby taking on a transnational function. These regulatory webs often do not depend on 'hard' international law, but on softer forms of governance that rely on – and in fact, require – the active participation of networks and agencies within the state. It is not hard or soft regulation that is significant then, but the potential that these regulatory webs create for the development of policy networks which act to release a particular regulatory project onto the variegated institutional landscapes of regional governance. The study of these networks can benefit the regional governments by assisting in the process of 'building' an IO region, and shaping it in a manner which does not over-burden the potential of such cooperative ventures. Our regulatory regionalism approach cannot, however, be conflated into a purely contextual approach, simply depending on the view or lens of each object-subject. Katzenstein's purely socially constructed version of regionalisms takes this post-modern turn too far. Katzenstein writes:

> "Regional designations are no more "real" in terms of geography than they are "natural" in terms of culture. Geography is not destiny. In the 1990s "the West" encompasses, among others, Western Europe and the United States as well as Canada, New Zealand and Australia, and, on many dimensions, Japan. Relatedly, "the Islamic world" does not describe a specific geographic location in the Mideast. It stretches from Indonesia to Nigeria and Northern Africa. As products of culture and economics, history and politics, geographically defined regions change over time".[20]

Whilst accepting the general point that often different types of regions are largely socially-constructed, we argue that the regional case for the Indian Ocean is stronger, and has an essential, non-human basis. Whilst recognising the contextuality of the region, this research project is premised upon an understanding that the Indian Ocean exists in *real ecospheric* terms. The region is defined as a grouping of those states which are touched by the waters of the Indian Ocean. To acknowledge and understand this form of *maritime regionalism* is essential when wrestling with the challenges which environmental and human security issues provide.

Any work which seeks to both analyse and promote IO regionalisms must move beyond investigations of exclusively nation-state actors. Many sub-national governments are now dealing directly with both nation-states (largely outside the view and control of their own nation-states), other sub-national governments, regional bodies, and non-state actors. Again, and in very final conclusion, let me revisit an earlier theme which initially led me to this research area – the importance of civic and non-state actors in initiating and truly driving regional policy-making and cooperative dialogues. Non-state, more informal politics are (and have been) already taking place across the region – states simply formalise and legitimate (at the very least) current political networks. At worst, they provide hindrances to the operations of these relationships, and, at best, they enable these more informal networks to flourish into truly creative regional partnerships.[21]

END NOTES

1. Kevin Rudd, speech at University of Western Australia: Australia's Foreign Policy Looking West, Perth, 12 November 2010, http://www.foreignminister.gov.au/speeches/2010/kr_sp_101112.html, accessed on 15 February 2010.
2. Tim Doyle and Melissa Risely, eds., *Crucible for Survival: Environmental Security and Justice in the Indian Ocean Region*, Rutgers University Press, New Brunswick, New Jersey and London, 2008, pp. 1-10.
3. Sanjay Chaturvedi, "Common Security? Geopolitics, Development, South Asia and the Indian Ocean," *Third World Quarterly,* vol. 19, no. 4, 1998, p. 712.
4. Dennis Rumley and Sanjay Chaturvedi, eds., *Energy Security and the Indian Ocean Region*, South Asian Publishers, New Delhi, 2005, pp. 1-5.
5. P.V. Rao, ed. *Regional Cooperation in the Indian Ocean: Trends and Prospects,* South Asian Publishers, New Delhi, 2001.
6. Andrew Hurrell, "Explaining the Resurgence of Regionalism in World Politics," *Review of International Studies,* vol. 21, 1995, p. 332.
7. Dabelko, G.D. and Dabelko, D.D., "Environmental Security: Issues of Conflict and redefinition", Woodrow Wilson Environmental Change and Security Project Report, Issue 1, 1995, pp. 3-12.
8. Doyle and Risely, *Crucible for Survival: Environmental Security and Justice in the Indian Ocean Region*, 2008, ch. 1.

9. Dennis Rumley, *The Geopolitics of Asia-Pacific Regionalism in the 21st Century*, seminar on 'The role of Asia Pacific countries for the development in the 21st century – issues over economic liberalisation and political balance', The Centre for Australian Studies, Otemon Gakuin University, Japan, 10 December 2005.
10. Sam Bateman and Anthony Bergin, *Our Western Front: Australia and the Indian Ocean*, Canberra: Australian Strategic Policy Institute (ASPI), March 2010.
11. Kanishka Jayasuriya, "The Strange Death of the International Liberal Order", *Economic and Political Weekly*, XLV, vol. 2, pp. 75-85.
12. Saskia Sasseen, *Territory, Authority, Rights: From Medieval to Global Assemblages,* Princeton University Press, Princeton, 2006.
13. N. Smith, 'Scale', in R.J. Johnston, D. Gregory, G. Pratt, and M. Watts eds., *Dictionary of Human Geography*, Blackwell Oxford, 2000.
14. Doyle and Risely, *Crucible for Survival: Environmental Security and Justice in the Indian Ocean Region,* 2008.
15. Dennis Rumley, *The Geopolitics of Asia-Pacific Regionalism in the 21st Century*, 2005.
16. Robertson & Dale, quoted in Jayasuriya, K., "Regionalising the State: Political Topography of Regulatory Regionalism", *Contemporary Politics*, vol. 14, no.1, 2008, pp. 21-35.
17. Sally Weller, "Power and scale: The shifting geography of industrial relations law in Australia", *Antipode,* vol. 39, no. 5, 2007, pp. 896-919.
18. Jamie Gough, "Changing Scale as Changing Class Relations: Variety and Contradiction in the Politics of Scale", *Political Geography*, vol. 23, no. 2, 2004, pp. 185-211.
19. Weller, 2007 and Erik Swyngedouw, "Neither Global nor Local: 'Globalisation' and the Politics of Scale", in K.R. Cox ed., *Spaces of Globalisation: Reasserting the Power of the Local*, The Guildford Press, New York and London, 1997, pp. 137-166.
20. P.J. Katzenstein, "Regionalism in Comparative Perspective", *Cooperation and Conflict*, vol. 31, no. 2, 1996, pp.123-159.

REFERENCES

Bateman, Sam and Bergin, Anthony (2010), *Our Western Front: Australia and the Indian Ocean*. Canberra: Australian Strategic Policy Institute (ASPI), March.

Chaturvedi, S. (1998), "Common Security? Geopolitics, Development, South Asia and the Indian Ocean", *Third World Quarterly*, 19 (4).

Chaturvedi, S. (2009), "Indian Ocean", in R. Kitchin and N. Thrift (eds.), *International Encyclopaedia of Human Geography,* vol. 5, Oxford: Elsevier, pp. 344-351.

Diani, M. and McAdam, D (eds.) (2003), *Social Movements and Networks*, Oxford: Oxford University Press.

Doherty, B.J. and Doyle, T.J. (2011), Transnational Solidarities: Friends of the Earth International, Basingstoke: Palgrave Macmillan.

Doyle, T. and Risely, M. (eds.) (2008), *Crucible for Survival: Environmental Security and Justice in the Indian Ocean Region*, New Brunswick, New Jersey and London: Rutgers University Press.

Fontana, A. and Frey, J.H. (2000), "The Interview: From Structured to Negotiated Text" in *Handbook of Qualitative Research*, 2nd edn., Denzin, N.K. and Lincoln, Y.S. (eds.) London: Sage Publications.

Gough, J. (2004), "Changing Scale as Changing Class Relations: Variety and Contradiction in the Politics of Scale", *Political Geography*, 23 (2): 185-211.

Hurrell, A. (1995), "Explaining the Resurgence of Regionalism in World Politics", *Review of International Studies*, vol. 21, pp. 331-358.

International Energy Agency (IEA) (2009) *World Energy Outlook 2009*, Paris: OECD/IEA.

Jayasuriya, K. (2008), "Regionalising the State: Political Topography of Regulatory Regionalism", *Contemporary Politics* 14 (1): 21-35.

Jayasuriya, K. (2010), "The Strange Death of the International Liberal Order", *Economic and Political Weekly,* XLV(23): 75-85.

Katzenstein, P.J. (1996), "Regionalism in Comparative Perspective", *Cooperation and Conflict*, vol. 31, no. 2, pp.123-159.

Pearson, M. (2008), *The Indian Ocean,* London: Routledge.

Rao, P.V., ed. (2001), *Regional Cooperation in the Indian Ocean: Trends and Prospects,* New Delhi: South Asian Publishers.

Rudd, K. (2010), Speech at University of Western Australia: Australia's Foreign Policy Looking West, Perth, 12 Nov 2010, available at <http://www.foreignminister.gov.au/speeches/2010/kr_sp_101112.html> accessed 15 February 2010.

Rumley, D. (2005), *The Geopolitics of Asia-Pacific Regionalism in the 21st Century*, presented at a seminar on 'The role of Asia-Pacific countries for the development in the 21st century – issues over economic liberalisation and political balance', held at The Centre for Australian Studies, Otemon Gakuin University, Japan, 10 December 2005.

Rumley, D. and Chaturvedi, S., (eds.) (2004), *Geopolitical Orientations, Regionalism and Security in the Indian Ocean*, New Delhi: South Asian Publishers.

Rumley, D. and Chaturvedi, S., (eds.) (2005), *Energy Security and the Indian Ocean Region*. New Delhi: South Asian Publishers.

Sasseen, S. (2006), *Territory, Authority, Rights: From Medieval to Global Assemblages,* Princeton: Princeton University Press.

Smith, N. (2000), 'Scale', in R.J. Johnston, D. Gregory, G. Pratt, and M. Watts (eds.), *Dictionary of Human Geography*, Oxford: Blackwell.

Swyngedouw, E. (1997), "Neither Global nor Local: 'Globalisation' and the Politics of Scale", in K.R. Cox (ed.), *Spaces of Globalisation: Reasserting the Power of the Local*, New York and London: The Guildford Press, 137-166.

Tilly, C. (2002), *Stories, Identities and Political Change*, Oxford: Rowman and Littlefield.

United Nations (1983), *The Law of the Sea*, New York: United Nations.

Weller, S. (2007), "Power and Scale: The Shifting Geography of Industrial Relations Law in Australia', *Antipode,* 39 (5): 896-919.

Chapter 2

Regionalism: "How" Successful? Inadequacy of Theories

Uttara Sahasrabuddhe

Introduction

Regionalism as a political project has been a significant phenomenon in post-1945 international relations. The 1950s and 1960s witnessed the rise of many regional groups in different parts of the world – the European Economic Community (EEC) in Western Europe, the Organisation of African Unity (OAU) in Africa, the Organisation of Petroleum Exporting Countries (OPEC) in the Middle-East, and the Association of Southeast Asian Nations (ASEAN) in Southeast Asia, to name a few. The aims and objectives of each of these were different. Some were created primarily to enhance security, some for political objectives such as promoting the national liberation movements, while some other were economic cartels. The success of the EEC, among these, was quite spectacular, but the same was not repeated in other parts of the world. By the end of the seventies, many of these regional organisations had been considerably weakened. Since the mid and late 1980s, regionalism began to re-appear in different parts of the world. This 'second wave' of regionalism almost coincided with the rise of globalisation. The two decades after the end of the Cold War have seen a proliferation of regional organisations and groups. While existing organisations like the EEC and the ASEAN re-invented themselves and consolidated further, this period also witnessed the rise of new groups and organisations, e.g. the South Asian Association for Regional

Cooperation (SAARC), Mercosur (i.e. the Southern Common Market) and the Indian Ocean Region – Association for Regional Cooperation (IOR-ARC).

A number of IR scholars have sought to explain and analyse the phenomenon of regionalism. Theories of regional integration began to be developed since the time European integration began to evolve. Understandably, the initial theories sought to explain and analyse primarily European experience of regionalisation. As regionalism began to spread in other parts of the world, more theoretical explanations were offered. These theories claimed to avoid ethno-centric explanations of regional experience, thereby making comparisons possible as well as meaningful. These theories also offered criteria for 'successful' regionalism. In the above context, this chapter makes a review of various theories of regionalism and examines their limitations mainly in analysing regionalisation processes outside Europe.

Some Definitions

Terms that are used most often in the context of regionalism need to be defined at the outset. These are: region, regional cooperation, regional integration, regionalism and regionalisation. Region is primarily a geographical entity. It can be said to comprise of states having geographical contiguity with each other. However, geographical regions are often ill-defined and their boundaries, blurred. Perception of shared interests and/or identities can convert a geographical region into a political unit.

Scholars of regionalism have tended to distinguish between regional cooperation and regional integration. Cooperation implies measures taken to solve specific problems, be that for short-term or for long-term. Regional cooperation does not necessarily aim at creating a larger, supra-national entity. Regional integration, on the other hand, strives towards it. The presence of a supra-national decision-making body distinguishes regional integration from mere cooperation.[1]

Some contemporary analysts have made a distinction between regionalism and regionalisation.[2] Regionalism, according to them, indicates the urge for a regionalist order, a strategy or a programme. Regionalisation, as distinguished from regionalism, indicates the processes that lead to patterns of cooperation, integration, complementarity and convergence within a particular cross-national geographical space. Hettne and Soderbaum also introduce the term 'regionness' in the study of regionalism.[3] Regionness denotes the different levels of integration in a geographical unit. He identifies five levels of regionness, and argues that the evolution from an earlier stage of regionness to a latter is the consequence of the processes of regionalisation.

Theories of Regionalism

The theories of regionalism can be divided into two broad categories: those emanating from the liberal approach to International Relations (IR), and those from the realist approach. The transactionalist, functionalist, neo-functionalist and federalist theories originate from within the liberal approach. The intergovernmentalist theory and also the theory of Regional Security Complex (RSC) have their roots in the realist approach to IR.

(a) **Transactionalism:** This theory is associated with the work of Karl Deutsch.[4] It originates from the liberal assumption that states are capable of overcoming their parochial orientations, that they are capable of cooperating and can form organisations to promote peace. According to Deutsch, integration is linked to the sense of community among nation-states. It is also linked with the efforts to evolve institutionalised procedures that help to resolve social problems without recourse to physical force. Deutsch identifies two types of communities: pluralistic security communities and amalgamated security communities. The latter leads to the formal merger of previously independent units, like in case of the formation of the USA. The former exists when nation-states retain their sovereignty and national identity; but harmonise their policies to achieve common goals. This theory was based on collection of huge empirical data from European countries.

(b) **Functionalism:** Another theory rooted in liberal approach to international relations is David Mitrany's functionalist theory of integration.[5] Mitrany's theory was based on two assumptions: first, states can transcend differences, seek mutual interests and evolve a web of institutions managed by technical elites; second, states are interdependent and cannot alone solve their economic as well as social problems. However, Mitrany was not in favour of all-encompassing international organisations. He preferred 'functional' organisations over IGOs like the UN.

(c) **Neo-functionalism:** Ernst Haas was the leading figure who developed the neo-functionalist theory of integration.[6] Haas seeks to explain how and why states cease to be fully sovereign; how and why they voluntarily mingle with their neighbours so as to "lose factual attributes of sovereignty" while acquiring new techniques of resolving conflicts between themselves. National and regional elites, political parties, pressure groups and supra-national institutions are the key actors in the process of integration. Neo-functionalism argues that it is the expectation of gain or loss of these groups that becomes the driving force of the process of integration. Speaking about possible convergence of interests and goals and the possibility of co-ordinated policies to seek such goals, neo-functionalism too, is a theory that adheres to the broad liberal approach to international relations.

(d) **Federalism:** Not all federations are voluntary unions of previously independent states. However, the formation of the European Union resembles a federalist project. Creating a federation is getting advantage of larger geographical unit while maintaining as much independence as possible of the constituent units. Federalism is also about territorial division of powers, about dividing the policy areas between the two levels of governance.[7] Much of this can be applied to the process of European regionalisation.

(e) **Intergovernmentalism:** This theory emanates from structural realist approach developed by Kenneth Waltz. It, thus, argues that sovereign states pursue regional integration only when their national goals are compatible with the regional goals. This is not easy and often results in slow pace of integration. Regionalisation process involves a series of bargains among governments in the region. These bargains are difficult as states are reluctant to compromise their national interest in favour of a common regional goal or regional approach.[8]

(f) **Regional Security Complex Theory (RSCT):** This theory is based on the premise that most threats to security are confined to a geographically bound region. Hence, "security interdependence is normally patterned into regionally based clusters: security complexes".[9] A theory developed mainly by Barry Buzan and Ole Waever, it argues that to understand security, one needs to analyse both the global and regional levels as independent levels and also their interaction.

(g) **New Regionalism Theory (NRT):** In addition to the theories reviewed above, there is another theory, the newest interpretation

> of regionalism, namely the New Regionalism Theory. This theory does not emanate from either the liberal or the realist approach, but finds its origins in the Critical Theories of IR. Developed by Bjorn Hettne and some other European scholars to analyse the 'second wave' of regionalism, this theory goes beyond the liberal as well as realist approaches and uses some of the arguments of social constructivism. The core argument of this theory is based on the concept of 'regionness'. The term 'regionness' is used to indicate the different levels of integration in a geographical unit. There are five levels of 'regionness' which are explained as follows:[10] (i) A region as a geographical unit or *regional space*; (ii) Region as a social system or *regional complex*; (iii) A region as transnational cooperation or *regional society*; (iv) A region as civil society or *regional community*; (v) A region as acting subject or *region state*.

Regionalism has implications for both security and development in a region.[11] In the first case, it aims at transforming "a security complex with conflict generating inter-state and intra-state relations" into "a security community with cooperative external relations and domestic peace". In the second case, it refers to "concerted efforts from a group of countries within a geographical region to increase the complementarity and capacity of the total regional economy as well as finding the right balance between functions and territory". Based on the five levels of regionness and the success of security and development regionalism, the different regions can be classified into three categories, namely, core regions, intermediate regions and peripheral regions.[12]

Limitations of the Theories in Rating Success/Failure of Regionalism

The theories discussed above can be applied to the regional experiences in various parts of the world. Thus, while exploring whether IOR-ARC is successful, most liberal theories of regionalism would look at aspects such as existence of institutionalised procedures at the supra-national level, or transfer of a part of the sovereign power of the member-states to the supra-national body. It can be said from the perspective of the transactionalist theory that IOR-ARC has not been able to evolve institutionalised procedures for resolving conflicts, and hence, is not successful regionalism. Or, from the neo-functionalist perspective, IOR-ARC is not successful because there is no loss of 'factual attributes of sovereignty' of member-states. The intergovernmentalist theory, rooted in realist paradigm, can offer explanations for a lack of success of IOR-ARC regionalism, namely, pace of regional integration in IOR-ARC is slow because bargains among member-states over how to make their respective national interest compatible with the larger interest of the IOR are not very successful. According to the New Regionalism Theory, IOR-ARC would be a case of peripheral regionalism due to the fact that regionness in IOR has not developed beyond the first level, i.e. regional space.

However, it may be noted here, that while the judgements rendered by these theories may (or may not) be correct, the causal explanations offered for those judgements may not do justice to the regional experiences outside Europe. This is primarily because, whether or not these theories claim European regionalism to be a *model*, they inadvertently assume the European *route* to it as *the route* to successful regionalism. They compare (a) regional experiences in terms of making of transnational organisations and building of transnational institutions, leading subsequently to the creation of supra-national communities, (b) the tenacity of that larger, supra-national entity, thus assuming the erosion of sovereignty or transfer of a part of decision-making power to the larger unit, as the route to regionalism and (c) perceive regional integration, and not merely regional cooperation, as the test of successful regionalism. However, the post-independence states in the Third World continue to be extremely sensitive about any 'loss' of sovereign power of the state, real or perceived. Thus, regionalisation processes in these regions have been completely averse to any development that would in any manner bring about erosion of sovereignty of the states. To adapt the terms used by Amitav Acharya, regional experiences in the Third World are 'sovereignty-based', unlike the 'sovereignty-eroding' regionalism in Europe.[13] Regionalisation processes in these parts of the world aims at regional cooperation, but not necessarily regional integration. As a result, regional organisations that are the product of these processes always remain subordinated to the sovereign member-states. This is true also in case of the IOR-ARC.

Therefore, it may be analytically more useful to go beyond comparisons based on regional organisations and institutions and look at the 'ideas' and 'norms' of regionalism among different societies. This will not only make comparisons more meaningful but also provide meaningful criteria for analysing the success or failure of a certain regional experience. The ideas and norms of regionalism in non-European societies are different from those in Europe. Thus, regional cooperation in the Third World does not mean looking beyond national interest, but to enhance national interest through cooperation among regional states. In the context of security, Third World regionalisms may not necessarily aim at resolving disputes, but may be content with avoiding conflicts within the region. In the context of economy and development, Asian states accept the idea of 'open' regionalism while Europe does not. Further, very often regional cooperation is viewed as a buffer against the forces of globalisation. Even in terms of norms, regionalism in Europe and elsewhere are quite different. While Europeans prefer institutionalised procedures of negotiation and decision-making, the Third World prefers backdoor negotiations and informal decision-making. They also prefer consensus-building over decision-making by majority.

Therefore, it is argued that it is useful to take a constructivist perspective while rating the success or failure of regionalisation process in a certain region. From this perspective, regional organisations emanate from the ideas of regionalism in a given region and are shaped by the norms of cooperation in that region. Specifically in case of the Third World, processes of regionalisation are shaped by the ideas of governments and the ruling elites (and not the people or society) on regionalism. The constructivist perspective makes possible inter-regional comparisons of the respective ideas and norms. It also makes possible to judge success or failure of a certain regionalisation process vis-a-vis its own ideas and norms (and not against some universal criteria). This may be illustrated with reference to the IOR-ARC.

Is IOR-ARC a Case of Successful Regionalism?

Like many other regional cooperation organisations in the Third World, the IOR-ARC does not aim at creating a robust supra-national entity, nor does it aim at evolving a 'community feeling' at the supra-national level. It aims at promoting cooperation, primarily economic, among the member-states. Its functional norms too, are similar to other regional organisations in the Third World: emphasis on informal negotiations to evolve a broad consensus over issues, and acceptance of open regionalism. The question whether the IOR-ARC is a case of successful regionalism will have to be answered with reference to its ideas and norms.

As regards the 'idea' of IOR-ARC, a few observations can be made:

(a) There is some ambivalence about the objectives of this regional organisation.

(b) Economic cooperation is a stated objective, but there is more beyond mere economic cooperation and that is not stated clearly, or perhaps that idea itself is not clear.

(c) It appears to be a group of countries concerned over the security of the IOR SLOCs – it also appears that they are concerned over domination of the IOR SLOCs by the extra-regional powers, however, there is no clear statement of these objectives.

(d) Some member-states, especially island countries seem to be concerned with the climate change and environmental damage and appear to make it an agenda of the IOR-ARC, but everyone does not seem to share these concerns.

A few issues about the functioning of the IOR-ARC may be noted:

(a) The group appears to lack in commitment on part of many of its members and this is reflected in the low frequency of meetings of the group.

(b) The significance of the group appears to be eroded by the simultaneous and parallel existence of several other regional organisations (such as ASEAN, ARF, EAS, BIMSTEC, SAARC, etc.) in the same region, which also deal with regional economic cooperation.

On the basis of the above, it can be said that the IOR-ARC is not a case of successful regionalism because lack of clarity of objectives as well as redundancy.

Concluding Remarks

The theories of regionalism are useful in analysing the phenomena of regionalism. However, most of them take an ethnocentric view of *the route* to regionalism. As a result, they fail to provide fair basis for comparisons as well as for rating the success of regionalisation processes in different parts of the world. A constructivist approach can be more useful in this respect. It may be worthwhile making inter-regional comparisons of ideas and norms; as well as rating success of a certain regional experience vis-a-vis its own ideas and norms.

END NOTES

1. Soren Dosenrode – "Regional Integration: Bringing the Classical Theories Back In?", *The IUP Journal of International Relations*, vol. IV, nos 1-2, January & April 2010, p. 11. Also see the discussion on 'regional interstate cooperation' and 'regional cohesion' by Andrew Hurrel, "Regionalism in Theoretical Perspective" in Lousie Fawcett & Andrew Hurrel (eds.), *Regionalism in World Politics: Regional Organisation and International Order*, Oxford University Press, New York, 1997, pp. 42-45.
2. Important among them are Bjorn Hettne and Fredrik Soderbaum. See Hettne and Soderbaum – "Theorising the Rise of Regionness" in Shaun Breslin, et. al. *New Regionalisms in the Global Political Economy: Theories and Cases*, Routledge, London, 2002, p. 34.
3. Ibid.
4. See Deutsch et. al. – *Political Community and the North Atlantic Area*, Princeton University Press, Princeton NJ, 1957.
5. David Mitrany – *A Working Peace System*, Chicago, Quadrangle, 1966.
6. Ernst Haas – *The Uniting of Europe*, Stanford University Press, Stanford, 1958
7. See Dosenrode, *op cit*. pp. 15-16.
8. The core argument of intergovernmentalism that the centrality of unitary state as the sole actors in IR was later criticised by the Interdependence Theory that was later expanded into neo-liberal institutionalism.
9. See Barry Buzan and Ole Waever – *Regions and Powers: The Structure of International Security*, Cambridge University Press, Cambridge: UK, 2003.
10. Hettne and Soderbaum, *op cit*.
11. Ibid.
12. Bjorn Hettne – "Globalism, Regionalism and the New Third World" in Nana Poku & Lloyd Pettiford (eds.) – *Redifining the Third World*, Macmillan, London, 1998.
13. For details, see Amitav Acharya – "Regionalism and the Emerging World Order: Sovereignty, Autonomy, Identity" in Breslin et. al. *op cit*.

Chapter 3

Regionalism: The Experience of the South-West Indian Ocean Islands

Christian Bouchard and William Crumplin

Introduction

In the South-West Indian Ocean (SWIO), four island states and three French island territories form a distinct and original regional community. These are the Union of the Comoros, the Republic of Madagascar, the Republic of Mauritius, the Republic of Seychelles, the French overseas departments of Mayotte and Réunion, as well as the French Scattered Islands in the Indian Ocean[1] (Figure 1). In this area of the Indian Ocean region, regional cooperation can best be portrayed as a multidimensional web of bilateral and multilateral relations between the governments, public institutions and local authorities, private economic operators and non-governmental organisations (NGO). Thus, the island governments are far from being the only actors involved in this cooperation, but it is assumed that they play a key role as regional cooperation falls into the realm of international affairs. Governments can and are also expected to exercise leadership in the development of regional relations.

This chapter attempts to investigate, in the context of the SWIO islands, the different processes of regionalism occurring concurrently as well as the multilateral cooperation taking place through regional organisations (ROs) and other main cooperation initiatives. Driven by economic globalisation, the global quest for sustainable development and generalised aspirations to create a more peaceful and secure world, there is a rising need for neighbouring countries to deepen their

Figure 1. The political map of the South-West Indian Ocean

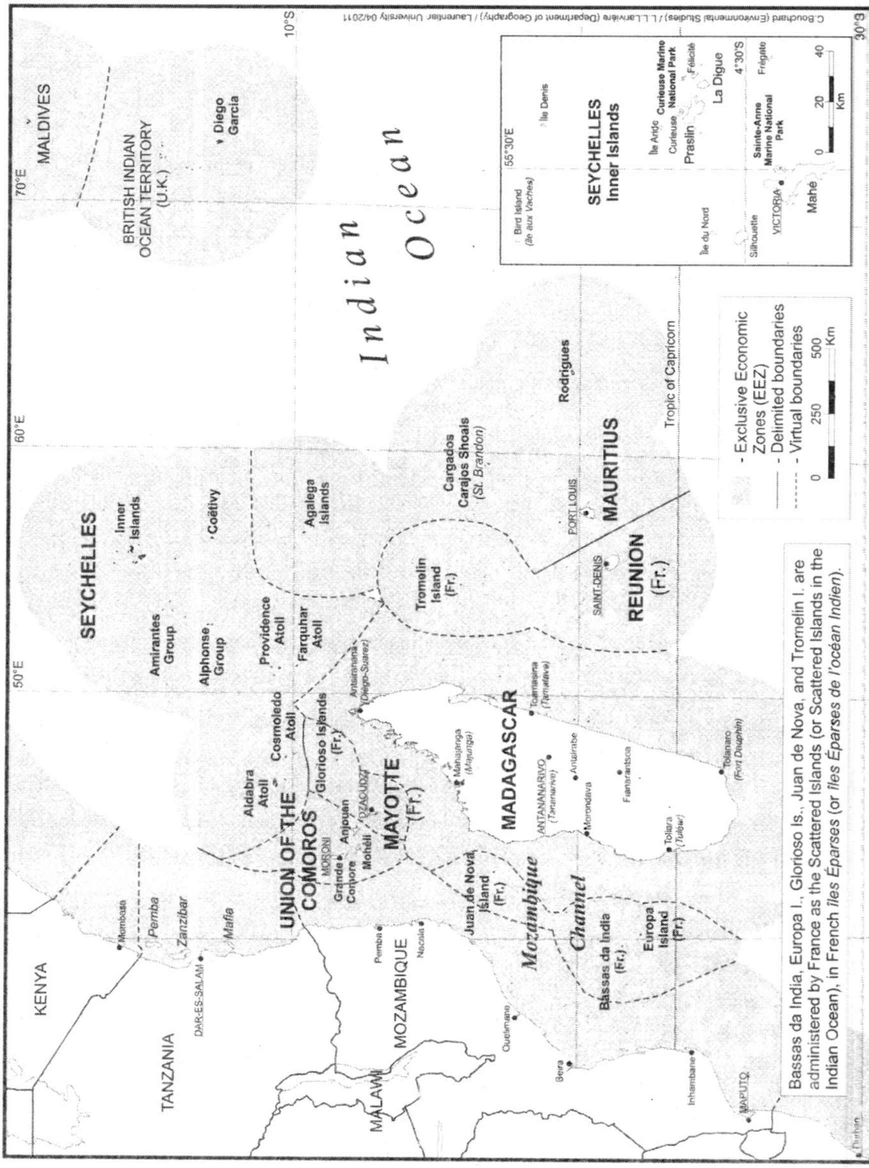

collaborative actions and this fosters regional cooperation and regional integration.[2] Our approach is more practical than theoretical as regional integration is understood as the building of a regional system from numerous and various linkages and developed at a specific geographical scale.

From the SWIO islands' perspective, three geographical levels of regionalism are witnessed. The first is the island community level which corresponds to the island-based cooperation and regional integration. The second is the intermediate level which links the islands to Eastern and Southern African countries in the emerging Region of Eastern and Southern Africa and the Indian Ocean (ESA-IO). The third is the continental and ocean-wide level, which links the islands to their broader relevant political, historical and socio-economical contexts, namely Africa and the Indian Ocean Region. This latter level is also the level of regional integration with Europe for Réunion and now Mayotte. Thus, the SWIO islands are involved in different processes of regionalism that are occurring simultaneously. All these processes, represented by the circle (the island community level) and the ovals (the other two geographical levels) drawn in Figure 2, are distinctive, intensifying and produce some coherence and regional identity.

In this context, the existing regional organisations (ROs) represent both the institutional means of regional cooperation as well as a very tangible sign of the regional integration processes underway. The ROs involving the SWIO islands are the Indian Ocean Commission (IOC), the Southern African Development Community (SADC), the Common Market for Eastern and Southern Africa (COMESA), the African Union (AU), the Indian Ocean Rim Association for Regional Cooperation (IOR-ARC), and the European Union (EU) in the case of Réunion and Mayotte (Table 1). However, these regional organisations are far from being the only relevant multilateral groupings as the islands also participate in, amongst others, the United Nations (UN) and institutions of the UN system (World Bank, UNDP, UNESCO, FAO, WHO, WTO, etc.), the Alliance of Small Island States (AOSIS) and the International Organisation of the French-speaking World (OIF). In addition, some strong bilateral relations within regional neighbours and with distant foreign powers are also of great importance to the islands, the most important being globally realised with France and other EU partners,

Figure 2. Processes of regionalism, main other multilateral groupings and main bilateral relations for the South-West Indian Ocean islands

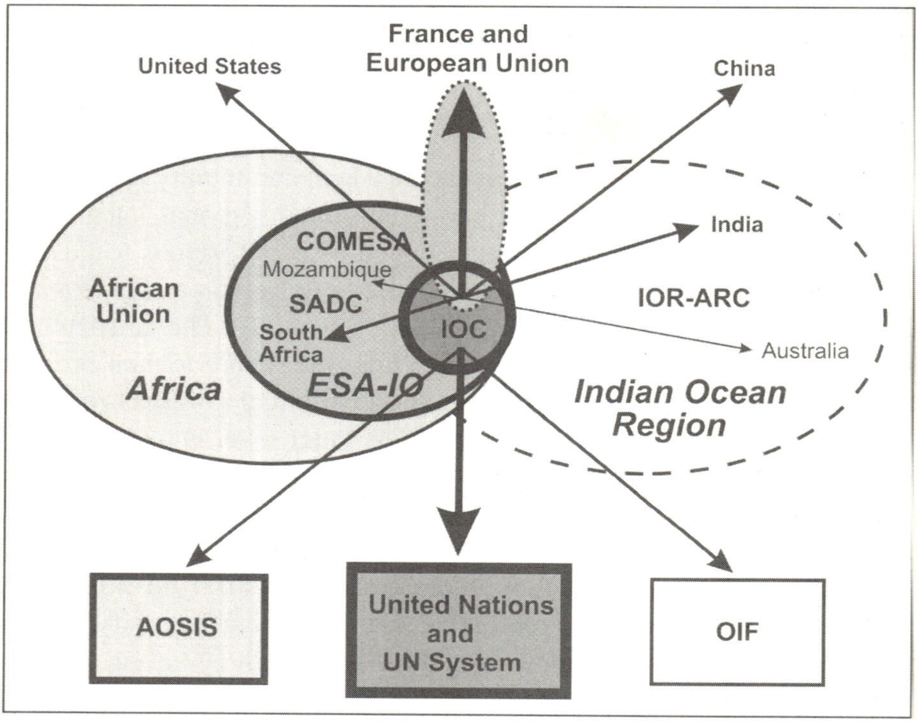

India, China, the United States and South Africa, as well as, on a lesser extent with Australia and Mozambique. Thus, regional cooperation is only one feature of the international system into which the states operate and interact, but it is a very significant feature that enhances the relations between neighbouring states at various geographical scales.

Our assessment of regional cooperation and regional integration involving the SWIO islands shows that the different ongoing processes of regionalism are not exclusive and, therefore, there is no contradiction for the islands to identify themselves as belonging to and participating in each of the corresponding regions. It is in this general context that we can understand the large number of regional organisations and other regional multilateral cooperation initiatives that involve the SWIO islands and that overlap in this area of the world. With this in mind, we propose to portray how the SWIO islands are involved in intergovernmental regional cooperation and regional integration by

Table 1. Membership of the SWIO Islands in Regional Organisations

	COM	MAD	MAU	MAY	RUN	Sc. Is	SEY	France
Indian Ocean Commission (IOC)	X	X	X	—	(France)	—	X	For Réunion
Common Market for Eastern and Southern Africa (COMESA)	X	X	X	—	—	—	X	Observer
Southern African Development Community (SADC)	—	X	X	(France)	(France)	—	X	IPC (c)
African Union (AU)	X	X	X	—	—	—	X	—
Indian Ocean Rim-Association for Regional Cooperation (IOR-ARC)	—	X	X	(France)	(France)	—	(1999-2003)	Dialogue Partner
European Union (EU)	—	—	—	(2014) (a)	X (b)	—	—	X

COM: Comoros. MAD: Madagascar. MAU: Mauritius. MAY: Mayotte. RUN: Réunion. SEY: Seychelles.

Sc. Is: Scattered Islands. (a) Should become integral part of the EU in 2014 when it acquires the status of EU's outermost region. (b) As an EU's outermost region. (c) International Cooperating Partner (IPC).

tackling the situation at the three different geographical levels of regionalism, beginning at the island community level, following with the intermediate level of the Region of Eastern and Southern Africa and the Indian Ocean, and finishing by the continental and ocean-wide level (Africa, Indian Ocean, Europe).

The SWIO island-based regionalism

Located off the African south-east coast, the islands of the South-West Indian Ocean forms a distinct sub-region of both Africa and the Indian Ocean Region. Two main factors contribute to their relative individualisation as a quite coherent regional community. The first is their island nature which, among other things, results in their physical isolation from their continental neighbours. Second, is their strong historic and continuing links to France, which still represents a very influential and leading regional player. However, this regional community remains very heterogeneous as each island entity possesses its unique mix of political, environmental, social and economic characteristics (Table 2, Appendix A), thereby making regional integration more complicated as the individual situations and priorities of each island are quite different.

In particular, the regional setting is characterised by the existence of different political status (independent states and French territories) as well as by the persistence of several territorial conflicts; two features that find their roots in colonial history and can hamper regional cooperation. While Comoros, Madagascar, Mauritius and Seychelles are now independent states, Mayotte, Réunion and the Scattered Islands are still under French sovereignty. Réunion became a French overseas department in 1946 (as well as a French region in 1982) while Mayotte just achieved overseas department and region status on 31 March 2011, having evolved from being a territorial collectivity of the Republic[3] (1976-2001) and departmental collectivity of the Republic[4] (2001-11). Unlike Réunion and Mayotte, the Scattered Islands are considered as simple dependencies as they remain outside of the French state's integral area (and thus are not part of the European Union).[5] Nevertheless, decolonisation has brought controversies and territorial disputes as the Comoros claims Mayotte and Banc du Geyser (in the Glorioso Islands' EEZ), Madagascar claims Bassas da India, Europa Island, Glorioso

Table 2. Synthesized Profiles of the South-West Indian Ocean Islands

		COM	MAD	MAU	MAY	RUN	SEY	Sc. Is
Political Status	State	X	X	X			X	
	Territory				X	X		
	Dependency							X
Territory Area	Small	X		X	X	X	X	X
	Medium							
	Large		X					
Population	Very Small				X		X	(a)
	Small	X		X		X		(a)
	Medium							(a)
	Large		X					(a)
Main Cultural Attributes	Creole			X		X	X	(a)
	French	(b)	(b)	(c)	X	X	(b)	(a)
	Indian			X		X		(a)
	Malagasy		X					(a)
	Swahili	X			X			(a)
Human Development Index	Low	X	X					(a)
	Medium							(a)
	High			X	X		X	(a)
	Very High					X		(a)
Economic Profile	LDC	X	X					(a)
	In transition				X			(a)
	Developed			X		X	X	(a)

COM: Comoros. MAD: Madagascar. MAU: Mauritius. MAY: Mayotte. RUN: Réunion. SEY: Seychelles. Sc. Is: Scattered Islands. LDC: Least Developed Countries. (a) Not applicable. (b) French is one of the official languages. (c) French is widely used in business and communication.

Islands, and Juan de Nova Island, and Mauritius[6] claims Tromelin Island. Thus, and despite its identification as a country/territory under foreign occupation by the African Union in 2004,[7] Réunion is the only French island of the region over which France sovereignty is not contested by any island state neighbour.[8]

At the island community level, the islands' interactions are very significant firstly on a bilateral basis. However, multilateral cooperation exists and is formalised by the Indian Ocean Commission, an inter-governmental organisation established in 1984[9] by the General Victoria Agreement. Its members are Comoros, Madagascar, Mauritius, Seychelles, and France/Réunion (France being represented by French state officials as well as by representatives of the two Réunion elected councils: the General Council – administering the Département de La Réunion, and the Regional Council – administering the Région Réunion). The original goals of the Commission were to strengthen the friendly links and solidarity between the peoples of the region as well as to promote economic development. With time, its missions evolved as new needs arose from its members and significant progress was made by both SADC and COMESA in regards to economic integration in the area. Today, the IOC defines itself as sub-regional organisation dedicated to the defence of the islands' interests, taking into account that its members share common development constraints (geographical isolation, small market size, environmental fragility, and high vulnerability to natural disasters) as well as a common identity and a tradition of solidarity.[10] Currently and emanating from the Third Summit of the Heads of State or Government held in Madagascar in 2005, the IOC is following four new strategic orientations:

(a) Political and diplomatic cooperation that pursues the goals of promoting regional stability and good governance, establishing the presence of the organisation on the international scene, as well as serving as the body to identify a common position for the defence of regional interests and economies;

(b) Economic and commercial cooperation that is expected to facilitate the integration of its members into the developing economic integration processes of the Region of Eastern and Southern Africa and of the Indian Ocean (ISA-IO Region);

(c) Regional sustainable development that focuses on the protection of the people and of their quality of life, as well as the protection and preservation of land and marine natural resources; and

(d) Regional cultural identity that will be strengthened by increasing linkages between the islands' peoples through the intensification of cultural exchanges as well as exchanges between professionals, women and youth organisations, reinforcement of academic and research cooperation, and a better circulation of people and ideas.

The IOC encountered problems in its first 20 years of existence, partly due to recurrent functioning difficulties and a lack of ambition.[11] Since the aforementioned Third Summit in 2005, the IOC has matured and is now reinvigorated. For instance, while IOC programmes accounted for some 100 million Euros from 1984 to 2005, its programmes for the 2005 to 2014 period will account for more than 200 million Euros, which represents a fourfold increase in the association's budgeted activities from the first to the second of these periods (doubling spending over a period half as long).[12] New programmes starting and to be realised in the coming years are related to fisheries, small island developing states, sustainable agriculture and adaptation to climate change, strengthening and valorisation of research, reduction of natural disaster's impacts, study and conservation of cetaceans and dugongs, developing a regional tool for audio-visual cooperation, peace and security, inter-island connectivity, maritime transportation, early warning capacities, and regional food security.

Four main developments contribute to the reinvigoration of this regional cooperation and improve its recognition in broader regional structures and on the international scene. First, acknowledging that it was not able to develop strong economic cooperation between members of different political status and between so different and weakly linked economies, the organisation positioned itself as a facilitator for its members to integrate with SADC and COMESA which works with the EAC towards the creation of a tripartite single free-trade agreement for the entire Eastern and Southern Africa area. Secondly, acknowledging that its members share many development constraints associated with small islands, the organisation positioned itself as the coordinator for the AIMS group (Africa, Indian Ocean, Mediterranean, and South China Sea) of the Small Island Developing States (SIDS). Thirdly, in the wake of continuing but evolving relations between the European Union and the ACP Group of States (Africa, Caribbean and Pacific), the IOC has now to negotiate its share of the Indicative Programme of Community Aid in favour of the ESA-IO Region with COMESA, EAC and IGAD. On this last point, the IOC also supports the action of the CMMR Group (Comoros, Madagascar, Mauritius and Seychelles) that actively participates in the negotiation of the Economic Partnership Agreement (EPA) between the European Union and the countries of Eastern and

Southern Africa (COMESA). Fourthly, recognising that regional cooperation represents a very efficient tool to cope collectively with common issues as well as to share costs and expertise, the IOC is willing to take advantage of every funding opportunity made available to developing states in matters of development and environment (including climate change adaptation) in addition to cooperating with other IGOs (for example: World Bank, UNICEF and IFAD) or NGOs (for example: WWF) when feasible.

However, due to unresolved territorial disputes, the SWIO island-based regional integration process remains incomplete as Mayotte and the Scattered Islands are not represented at the IOC or included in its programmes. This is a serious problem for Mayotte, which is now looking for better regional integration, but is still limited due to weak relations with its neighbours. Officially launched in 2003, with the support of the Regional Cooperation Fund (provided by the French state), Mayotte's first regional cooperation actions have been successful[13] and its regional cooperation will continue to develop in the wake of its new overseas department and region status and of its future EU outermost region status that it should acquire in 2014. Nevertheless, Mayotte can not join the IOC without the approval of Comoros that continues to claim firmly and loudly that Mayotte is not French but Comorian. This is a lingering issue dating back to 1975 and it would be very surprising if this issue is resolved in the foreseeable future. However, Mayotte has been able to participate for the first time in the last Indian Ocean Island Games held in Madagascar in 2007, and will participate again in the next games to be presented in Seychelles in August 2011.[14] This is only a small step towards better regional integration, but it is recognition that the Mahorais people are legitimate members of the SWIO island community.

In regards to the Scattered Islands, France proposed a co-management scheme for the islands by the disputing countries, a principle that was agreed upon at the IOC's Second Summit of the Heads of State and Government in 1999. However, the islands remain outside of the IOC regional cooperation agenda and the co-management is to be achieved through bilateral relations. Such bilateral relations are the basis for the agreement of 7 June 2010, between France and Mauritius on their common management of high sea fisheries, environmental protection and archaeological research in Tromelin Island.[15] Nevertheless, France is very willing to develop regional cooperation actions involving the Scattered Islands,[16] especially on maritime transportation, meteorological services, high sea fisheries, and environment and biodiversity protection, but this cooperation can not be accomplished inside of the IOC framework.

Overall, despite some difficulties in the past and remaining issues in regards to the situations of Mayotte and the Scattered Islands, multilateral cooperation has become an important feature at the island community level. New local needs for cooperation (as shown by the list of ongoing programmes at the IOC), as well as new cooperation dynamics at higher geographical levels (for example: economic integration of the ESA-IO Region, AOSIS and SIDS issues) has brought the Indian Ocean Commission to revise its strategic orientations accordingly so it can now successfully both expand its own cooperation programme agenda and better represent its members in higher levels of regional integration and on the international scene. Finally, the establishment and the recent reinvigoration of the IOC contribute highly to cultivate a common regional island-based identity, as well as demonstrating the islanders' will to promote co-development, perpetuate existing friendly links and continue to build solidarity. As a strong symbol of this, the IOC will most probably change its name soon for Indian Ocean Community (in French *Communauté de l'Océan Indien*).[17]

The Region of Eastern and Southern Africa and the Indian Ocean

From the SWIO islands' perspective, the second geographical level of regional integration is with the emerging and quickly developing Region of Eastern and Southern African and the Indian Ocean (ESA-IO Region); the term "Indian Ocean" here is a synonym for the SWIO islands. In this case, regional cooperation is realised through several regional organisations that are themselves cooperating together on ESA-IO issues, such as a tripartite free-trade agreement and multilateral relations with the European Union. In addition to the IOC, these ROs include COMESA, EAC, IGAD and SADC. Therefore, there are two different scales of regional cooperation at this intermediate level of regionalism. First, we find a standard multilateral cooperation characterising each of the individual regional organisations; this is the island community level discussed above with the case of the Indian Ocean Commission. Second, we find an existing web of cooperation between regional organisations that also allow the participation of individual state members or subgroups of state members. As a consequence, the SWIO islands are seen to be first participating in the IOC, COMESA and SADC to which most of them are members (Table 3), but they are also fully involved in the ESA-IO region-wide cooperation as individual parties as well as collectively through the Indian Ocean Commission which is also very much involved in this emerging regional integration process.

Table 3. Regional Economic Commissions (SADC, COMESA, EAC, IGAD) and other Economic Agreements (SACU, COMESA FTA) in the Region ESA-IO Region

	SADC	SACU	COMESA	COMESA FTA	EAC	IGAD
Angola	X		X			
Botswana	X	X				
Burundi			X	X	X	
Comoros			**X**			
D.R. of the Congo[(a)]	X		X			
Djibouti			X	X		X
Egypt[(b)]			X			
Eritrea			X			X
Ethiopia			X			X
Kenya			X	X	X	X
Lesotho	X	X				
Libya[(b)]			X			
Madagascar	**X**		**X**	**X**		
Malawi	X		X	X		
Mauritius	**X**		**X**	**X**		
Mayotte (France)	**(France)[(d)]**		**(France)[(e)]**			
Mozambique[(c)]	X					
Namibia	X	X				

Table 3 (Contd.)

	SADC	SACU	COMESA	COMESA FTA	EAC	IGAD
Réunion (France)	**(France)[(d)]**		**(France)[(e)]**			
Rwanda			X	X	X	
Seychelles			**X**			
Somalia						X
South Africa	X	X				
Sudan			X	X		X
Swaziland	X	X	X			
Tanzania	X				X	
Uganda			X		X	X
Zambia	X		X	X		
Zimbabwe	X		X	X		

Note: SWIO islands underlined in bold. (a) D.R.Congo participates in the Central Africa EPA negotiations (CEMAC/CEEAC). (b) Egypt and Libya participate to the Euro-Mediterranean Partnership (EUROMED). (c) Mozambique is considering joining SACU. (d) France has the status of International Cooperating Partner at SADC. (e) France has an observer status at COMESA.

The region-wide regionalism is firstly economically driven, but elements of cooperation extend to political, social and environmental matters. Overall, this regional economic integration process represents a concrete step towards the convergence of the eight regional economic commissions recognised by the African Union (in accordance with the Accra Declaration, 9th African Summit, July 3, 2007).[18] Regional integration policies should contribute to this objective by promoting the cohesion, unity and economic integration of the ESA-IO region.[19] It is in this context that a tripartite negotiation has been established to achieve an enlarged free-trade area covering the SADC, COMESA and the EAC, and thus, by default, all four IOC island states as they are COMESA members (France/Réunion has an observer status at COMESA and is following this free-trade initiative with attention). As a result, until the African Union's envisioned African Common Market and African Economic Community[20] are fully realised, the ESA-IO Region now appears to be the desirable geographical level of economic integration for the SWIO island economies.

This ESA-IO integration process is also very much strengthened by the two main mechanisms governing the very unique cooperation between the European Union and the ACP Group of states, namely the Economic Partnership Agreements[21] (EPAs) and the Regional Indicative Programmes[22] (RIPs). At the ESA-IO level, three interim EPAs have been negotiated between the EU and some COMESA members (Mauritius, Seychelles, Zimbabwe and Madagascar) as well as with SADC and EAC. Instead of one single EPA for the entire ESA-IO region as initially planned, negotiations continue to achieve individual comprehensive EPAs with COMESA, EAC and SADC. Nevertheless, a single EPA may well be possible when the tripartite free-trade agreement is realised. The RIP for the ESA-IO Region (2008-2013) supports this development and represents a general allocation of some 645 million Euros in financial aid to be shared between COI, COMESA, EAC and IGAD. These allocated funds are slated to be distributed as follows:[23]

(a) Regional economic integration (including infrastructure and energy, as well as natural resources, environment and food security): 85 per cent of the total allocation (€548 million);

(b) Regional political integration/cooperation (conflict prevention, peace and security, post-conflict reconstruction, dialogue on governance and security): 10 per cent of the total allocation (€64 million); and

(c) Other programmes (knowledge development and capacity building, capacity development of the regional organisation and inter-regional coordination): 5 per cent of the total allocation (€32 million).

Even if these programmes do not dovetail perfectly, they have been conceived to bring more coherence to and develop a stronger economic framework in the ESA-IO Region; as well they will contribute to political stability, human development and sustainable development. These programmes target the area largely covered by the four regional economic commissions involved in the region-wide integration, namely SADC, COMESA, EAC and IGAD (Table 3). This area, covering about half of the African states (twenty-five states[24]) plus the French SWIO islands, represents a total of about 525 million inhabitants (mid-2011), a GDP of about 1200 billion $US in purchasing power parity (2010), and exports of some 180 billion $US (2010), for which the SWIO islands only respectively represents 4.8, 5.1 and 2.3 per cent.[25] As a consequence, the challenge for the SWIO islands is to integrate into this larger and massive region while being able, at the same time, to defend their specific economic situations and development needs.

At the same time, that economic integration will progress region-wide, regional organisations will remain very useful structures for the management of various cooperation programmes at their own geographical scale (as seen by the IOC example), and thus there is no contradiction between the co-existence of the island community and intermediate level regionalisms. Outside the formal ROs framework, other important regional initiatives already operate in the same region, but focus on maritime issues instead of on land-based matters. This is consistent with environmental, socio-economical and political factors that tend to create some coherence within the Indian Ocean maritime area off the African coasts, from Somalia in the north to South Africa at the southern tip of the continent. In terms of state maritime areas (territorial sea, contiguous zone, exclusive economic zone, and continental shelf), and contrary to their regional small weight in terms of population, GDP and exports, the contribution of the SWIO islands to the regional total is very significant. Altogether, with a total area of some five million sq km, the combined territorial seas and exclusive economic zones of Comoros, France, Madagascar, Mauritius and Seychelles account for half of the region's total area and, therefore, represent and include vast potential in terms of marine resources. The importance of the SWIO islands for maritime-based cooperation in the ESA-IO region is also greatly enhanced by the fact that they represent more or less half of the participating coastal states depending on the regional initiative considered (Table 4).

In regards to marine environment, marine living resources and fisheries, two main multilateral initiatives cover the area, namely: the Eastern African Regional Sea Programme (Nairobi Convention for the Protection, Management and Development of the Marine and Coastal Environment of the Eastern African Region),[26] and the Southwest Indian Ocean Fisheries Commission (SWIOFC).[27] Four other ongoing or recent important marine-oriented projects need to be acknowledged and include the Southwest Indian Ocean Fisheries Project (SWIOFP),[28] the Agulhas and Somali Current Large Marine Ecosystems Project (ASLME

Table 4. Maritime-oriented Regional Initiatives in the ESA-IO Region

	EA-RSP (Nairobi Convention)	**SWIOFC**	**SWIOFP**	**ASLME Project (2008-12)**	**ReCoMap (2006-11)**	**WIO-LaB**	**Second ERMMP (a)**
Comoros	**X**	**X**	**X**	**X**	**X**	**X**	**X**
Djibouti							X
France	**X**	**X**	**X**	**(observer)**		**X**	**X** [(c)]
Kenya	X	X	X	X	X	X	X
Madagascar	**X**	**X**	**X**	**X**	**X**	**X**	
Maldives		X					
Mauritius	**X**	**X**	**X**	**X**	**X**	**X**	**X**
Mozambique	X	X	X	X		X	
Seychelles	**X**	**X**	**X**	**X**	**X**	**X**	**X**
Somalia	X	X	(observer)	(observer)	X	X	X
South Africa	X	X	X	X		X	X
Tanzania	X	X	X	X	X	X	X
Yemen		X					

Note: SWIO islands states underlined in bold (France for Réunion, Mayotte and Scattered Islands). (a) ESA-IO states represented at the Second Regional Ministerial Meeting on Piracy and Maritime Security in the ESA-IO Region; in attendance were also representatives of COMESA, EAC, IGAD, IOC, SADC, Maldives, China, India, Pakistan, Russia, United States, United Nations, African Union, INTERPOL and IONS. (c) France/Réunion.

Project),[29] the just concluded Regional Coastal Management Programme of the Indian Ocean Countries (ReCoMap),[30] and the WIO-LaB Project (Project "Addressing Land-Based Activities in the Western Indian Ocean") which was managed by the Nairobi Convention Secretariat until it officially concluded on 30 June, 2010.[31] Finally, as maritime piracy has arisen as a new serious and challenging issue in the area, two Regional Ministerial Meetings on Piracy and Maritime Security in the ESA-IO Region (ERMMP) have already been held (May and October 2010) and it has been proposed that this forum becomes an annual event.

Thus, Eastern and Southern African and the Indian Ocean (ESA-IO) is definitively emerging today as a coherent area for regional cooperation and integration, whether it be for land-based or for maritime-oriented matters. In many ways, this enhances the links between Africa and the Indian Ocean, and the ESA-IO Region can be seen as the interface between these two larger worlds. At this geographical scale, an intermediate level of regionalism is developing fast while island community level regionalism continues to be pertinent. For the SWIO islands, successful integration to this intermediate level of regional cooperation is absolutely necessary in terms of both economic matters and maritime affairs.

The Regional Integration to Africa, Indian Ocean Region and Europe

The third and last geographical level of regionalism involving the SWIO islands is occurring at the continental and ocean-wide level and links the islands to their broader political, historical, environmental and socio-economic contexts. Contrary to the regional integration processes ongoing at the island community and intermediate scales, where the different dynamics of regional cooperation combine to strengthen the islands' integration to unique and well defined geographical areas (namely the SWIO island community and the Region of Eastern and Southern Africa and the Indian Ocean), we find a very different situation at the small or course-scale level of analysis. In this broader context, three different regional integration processes are operating simultaneously and link the SWIO islands to Africa, the Indian Ocean Region, and even Europe for Réunion and Mayotte. These three processes are not exclusive and therefore there is no contradiction for the islands to identify themselves as belonging to each of the corresponding regions.

Of these three course-scale regional integration processes, the easiest to deal with is the one linking the SWIO islands to Africa. As the islands are geographically considered African,[32] and in the wake of European colonisation that considered them as such, the four islands states very naturally joined the group of African states when they achieved independence (from France: Madagascar in 1960 and Comoros in 1975; from Great Britain: Mauritius in 1968 and Seychelles in 1976). The islands' political and economic integration in this continent-wide multilateral cooperation is realised through their membership in the African Union (AU) and in the African Economic Community (AEC). The linkage of the islands to Africa is now strengthened by their increasing integration to Eastern and Southern Africa in what we have described as the regional integration process of the ESA-IO Region. Apart from their strong political and economic relations with their continental neighbours, shared historical background and cultural linkages also greatly contribute to the African identity of the islands.

In regard to regional integration with Africa, the situation is definitively different for Réunion and Mayotte than for the four other island states. Réunion, as a French overseas department and region as well as being an EU outermost region,[33] is politically bound and geographically integrated into the European Union, a situation towards which Mayotte is fast evolving (French department in 2011, French region and EU outermost region in 2014). Since France is a European State and will not integrate in the AU and the AEC on behalf of its African island territories, this leave Réunion and Mayotte outside of the formal continental-wide political integration process. Nevertheless, Réunion (and most probably Mayotte in the coming years) is following the economic integration of the ESA-IO Region with great interest and looks forward to be associated with and to benefit from it. An innovative economic partnership between France/Réunion/Mayotte can certainly be envisaged once the tripartite COMESA-EAC-SADC free-trade agreement comes into existence. However, history and culture link both Mayotte and Réunion to the continent and both are developing bilateral relations with some continental states and local communities of Southern Africa.

As shown by the case of Réunion, sport can also serve as a linkage tool between the French territories and their continental African neighbours. For example, Réunion is an associate member of the Confederation of the African Football (CAF), and, as such, participates in most of the CAF competitions. In addition, as part of the French contribution, Réunion and Mayotte are also involved in the maritime-based cooperation ongoing in the ESA-IO Region (for example, in the SWIOFC). Thus, even if their situation is much different from their SWIO island state counterparts, Mayotte, as part of the Swahili world, and Réunion, which experienced slavery under French colonisation and is now developing new relations with the continent, are both involved in the general process of integration of the SWIO islands to Africa.

In regards to the Indian Ocean Region, the process of regional integration is in its initial stages and progress has been slow since the first region-wide initiative calling for an international Conference on the Indian Ocean in the wake of the UN Declaration of the Indian Ocean as a Zone of Peace (IOZP, 1971), a conference that was originally scheduled for 1981 but, in the end, never materialised. Nevertheless, there is an ongoing process of integration at the Indian Ocean-wide scale, and the SWIO islands are definitively part of this as they are fast developing their relations with other states of the region and claim an Indian Ocean identity. Currently, the islands' regional integration with the Indian Ocean Region is mainly realised through bilateral relations. However, some multilateral initiatives are leading the way towards stronger regional integration (Table 5) and these are discussed below.

Table 5. The Indian Ocean Rim States and the Main Current Indian Ocean-wide Regional Cooperation Initiatives

	IOR-ARC	IOTC (c) (d)	IONS (e)	IOGOOS (f)
Australia	X	X	X	X
Bangladesh	X		X	
Comoros		X	X	
Djibouti			X	
France	(a)	X	X	X
India	X	X	X	X
Indonesia	X	X	X	X
Iran	X	X	X	X
Kenya	X	X	X	X
Madagascar	X	X	X	X
Malaysia	X	X	X	
Maldives		(d)	X	
Mauritius	X	X	X	X
Mozambique	X		X	X
Myanmar (Burma)			X	
Oman	X	X	X	
Pakistan		X	X	
Seychelles	(b)	X	X	
Singapore	X		X	
Somalia				
South Africa	X	(d)	X	X
Sri Lanka	X	X	X	X
Tanzania	X	X	X	X

Table 5 (Contd.)

	IOR-ARC	IOTC (c) (d)	IONS (e)	IOGOOS (f)
Thailand	X	X	X	
Timor-Leste				
U.A.E.	X		X	
U.K. (BIOT)		X		
Yemen	X		X	

Note: (a) As a dialogue partner (as China, Egypt, Japan, United Kingdom, IOTO and IORG). (b) Seychelles joined IOR-ARC in March 1999, but withdrew in July 2003. (c) Other non-IORim members: Belize, China, Eritrea, European Union, Guinea, Japan, South Korea, Philippines, Sierra Leone, Sudan, and Vanuatu. (d) Maldives, Senegal, South Africa and Uruguay are cooperating non-contracting parties. (e) Membership made of navies and not states, other member-navies: Bahrain, Egypt, Eritrea, Kuwait, Qatar, Saudi Arabia, and Sudan. (f) Membership made of organisations/institutions and not states, one other member from the United States.

On the one hand, there are two main inter-governmental organisations operating in the Indian Ocean Region. First is the Indian Ocean Rim Association for Regional Cooperation (IOR-ARC)[34] that promotes intra-regional trade and investment, and it is now developing other areas of cooperation such as maritime transport, tourism, fisheries, as well as science and technology transfer. Second is the Indian Ocean Tuna Commission (IOTC)[35] that as been established to manage tuna and tuna-like species in the Indian Ocean and adjacent seas. Another regional organisation, the Indian Ocean Marine Affairs Co-operation (IOMAC),[36] was created in 1990, but has not rallied enough members to become a successful forum for region-wide cooperation. Finally, another regional project, the International Forum on the Indian Ocean Region (IFIOR) met in Perth in June 1995, but this second-track initiative also failed to develop momentum and was rapidly abandoned.

On the other hand, there are also other emerging and promising cooperation initiatives that enhance the coherence and the identity of the Indian Ocean as a region. For example, there is the Indian Ocean Navy Symposium (IONS)[37] tackling maritime security issues (first meeting in 2008) and the Indian Ocean Global Ocean Observing System (IOGOOS)[38] working on oceanography matters (established in 2002). Thus, after some hesitations and challenges in the last few decades or so, the Indian Ocean-wide regional integration is gaining importance and structure. Contrary to early cooperation initiatives (such as the IOZP Declaration of 1971 and the never organised UN Conference on the Indian Ocean, and the IOMAC Agreement of 1990) that were to broadly include littoral and hinterland states of the Indian Ocean and its tributaries (Indian Ocean Region), the current IOR-ARC initiative focus on the coastal states of the main body of the Indian Ocean, a geographical area recognised as the Indian Ocean Rim.

With no doubt, the SWIO islands are parties to this emerging ocean-centric regionalism and identify themselves strongly with the Indian Ocean Rim (IOR), the Indian Ocean Region and the Indian Ocean World (roughly including the Indian Ocean Region and sometimes extended to the entire South-East Asia and China). Even though the SWIO islands represent only a small share of the Indian Ocean Region's population and economy, they nevertheless are very important stakeholders in maritime affairs and especially with regard to living marine resources. In addition to multilateral cooperation, bilateral cooperation and economic relations are developing fast between the islands and some of the non African rim states, in particular with India with whom they share significant historical, cultural and even family links (mainly in the case of Mauritius and Réunion), and, to a lesser extent, with Australia. The latter is a main destination for higher education and professional training as well as a destination for immigrating islanders. As a result, and despite the fact the inter-governmental Indian Ocean-wide regional cooperation is not yet fully developed, the Indian Ocean Region is very important to the SWIO islands. Overall, taking into consideration that the ESA-IO Region is also included in the Indian Ocean Region, the importance of maritime matters in the emerging ocean-wide cooperation, as well as the very significant bilateral relations between the islands and some other coastal states, the SWIO islands integration with the Indian Ocean Region appears to be as significant for them as their integration with Africa.

Finally, compared to the regional integration of all the SWIO islands with Africa and the Indian Ocean Region, is the integration of Réunion and Mayotte to Europe or more precisely the European Union. Thus, the challenge for these two islands is to successfully cooperate with and integrate into their geographical environment (SWIO island community,

ESA-IO Region, Africa and Indian Ocean Region) while, at the same time, being integral parts of the French Republic and the European Union. Apart from the fact that Mayotte is somehow politically isolated as a result of the Comorian claim on the island, the political status of Réunion and Mayotte remain a problem as they cannot participate as equal members in the existing regional organisations of their geographical area. In addition, a second main challenge comes from their economic integration into France's and the EU's economies which are very different than their neighbours' economies. However, the European Union is also very important for the four SWIO island states in that they also realize very significant bilateral relations with EU members and multilateral relations with the EU are of chief importance (especially in regards to EPA and RIP). Therefore, at the same time as Réunion and now Mayotte are being formally integrated with the European Union, their four SWIO island neighbours are also deeply involved and committed to sustain cooperation with the EU and its members.

Conclusion

In some areas of the world, it seems that there is a profusion of different regional initiatives, tackling a vast array of issues of various nature (political, environmental, social, and economical, land-based or maritime-oriented), while operating at various geographical scales from the immediate neighbourhood to the much larger areas or regions. This is exactly what we find in the case of the South-West Indian Ocean islands. However, from this unique perspective, our analysis of regional cooperation shows that there is much consistency within specific geographical scales and we find three levels of regionalism: (1) the island community level which corresponds to island-based cooperation and regional integration, (2) the intermediate level which links the islands to the emerging Region of Eastern and Southern Africa and the Indian Ocean (ESA-IO), and (3) the continental and ocean-wide level which links the islands to Africa and the Indian Ocean Region, as well as Europe for Réunion and now Mayotte.

Thus, the SWIO islands are currently and simultaneously involved in five different processes of regional integration operating at three different geographical scales (Figures 2 and 3). These processes, driven by the existing regional organisations and other main regional

Figure 3. South-West Indian Ocean Islands and Regional Systems in the Indian Ocean Region

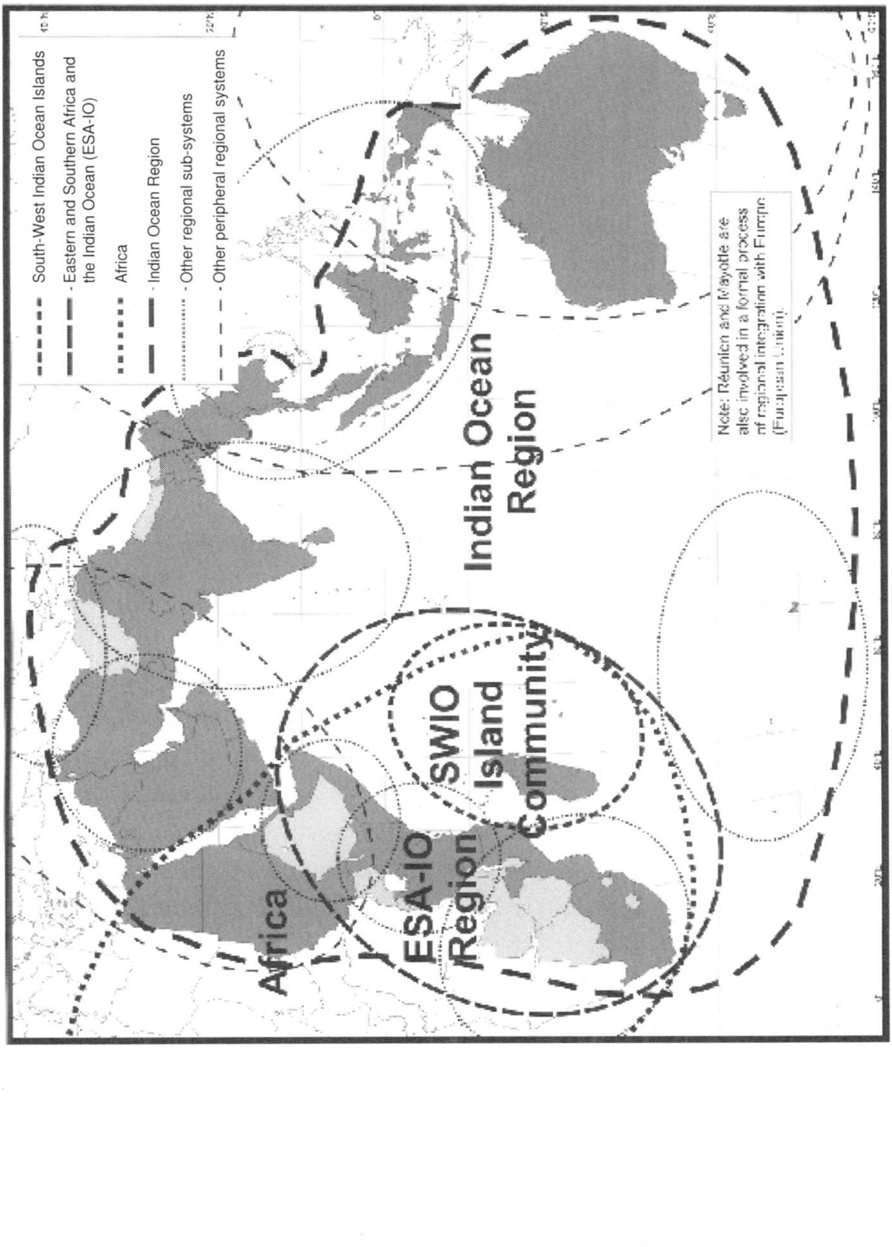

cooperation initiatives, generate some regional coherence and strengthen regional identities. As these processes of regional integration are not exclusive, there is no contradiction for the islands to identify themselves as belonging to and participating in each of the corresponding regions. It is in this general context that we can understand the large number of regional organisations and other regional multilateral cooperation initiatives that involve the SWIO islands and that overlap in this area of the world.

From the island community level, we highlight the challenge of developing strong regional cooperation between very different members, as well as illustrate how some political issues can complicate successful inclusive cooperation. In addition, the experience of the Indian Ocean Commission reminds us that it often takes some time before a regional organisation becomes really effective as it has to find the common ground between its members on which the cooperative efforts can prosper, as well as develop the right structures and relative budget allocations. From the intermediate level of the ESA-IO Region, we found that regional cooperation and even a process of regional integration can develop even if there is no specific regional organisation in place for that specific region. In this emerging region, regionalism is driven by economic integration and maritime cooperation realised by a large number of regional cooperation initiatives (tripartite FTA, EU-ESA-IO's RIP, EPAs, SWIOFC, Eastern African Regional Sea Programme, etc.) involving both regional organisations operating at the lower geographical level (IOC, SADC, COMESA, EAC, IGAD) and their individual state members.

From the continental and ocean-wide level, we find that the SWIO islands can simultaneously pursue regional integration with Africa, the Indian Ocean Region, and even Europe for Réunion and Mayotte, all being very pertinent to the islands. For the Indian Ocean Rim Association for Regional Cooperation (IOR-ARC), the challenge is to acknowledge other regional initiatives (such as IOTC, IOGOOS and IONS) and to develop its own areas of competence. Nevertheless, as regional cooperation and regionalism are far from being an exclusive state and regional organisation domains, an Indian Ocean Region process of regionalism does exist and can develop with or without the IOR-ARC. Based on a long history of economic and cultural ocean-wide relationships, there is definitively an Indian Ocean identity on which Indian Ocean regionalism can prosper; this could be enhanced greatly if the regional states can transcend some political issues and show the will to develop and pursue an agenda designed to promote cooperation on regional issues.

End Notes

1. Formed by the Bassas da India atoll, Glorioso Islands (which exclusive economic zone includes Banc du Geyser), Juan de Nova Island, Europa Island, and Tromelin Island, the Scattered Islands in the Indian Ocean (in French: *îles Éparses de l'océan Indien* or *îles Éparses*) constitute one of the five administrative districts of the French Southern and Antarctic Lands (in French: *Terres australes et antarctiques françaises*).
2. In its broader sense, regional integration is a process in which neighbouring countries establish formal cooperation (treaties/agreements/protocols, institutions/projects/standards) in order to cope collectively on issues of common concerns (including political, economical, environmental, social and/or cultural matters), promote peaceful relations and regional stability, enhance economic and human development, as well as develop regional coherence and identity.
3. In French: *Collectivité territoriale de la République*.
4. In French: *Collectivité départementale de la République*.
5. As a French overseas territory (see also note 1), the French Southern and Antarctic Lands (TAAF) possess the EU status of Overseas Countries and Territories (OCTs), and, therefore, are not part of the EU territory.
6. Mauritius also claims the Chagos Archipelago which is actually administered by the United Kingdom as the British Indian Ocean Territory.
7. African Union Commission, *Strategic Plan of the African Union Commission, Volume 1: Vision and Mission of the African Union*, Annex 3: List of African Countries/Territories under Foreign Occupation, 2004, p. 43.
8. Christian Bouchard, "France and United Kingdom as the 37th and 38th Indian Ocean Coastal States", *Indian Ocean Survey* (Indian Ocean Research Group), vol. 3, no. 1-2, 2007, pp. 36-52.
9. Following Port Louis Declaration, December 20, 1982, by Madagascar, Mauritius and Seychelles.
10. IOC, Official Webpage, "Des orientations stratégiques renouvelées", http://www.coi-ioc.org/index.php?id=42, accessed 7 April 2011.
11. Bertile, "Dans l'océan Indien, la richesse de l'intégration", *Le Monde Diplomatique*, March 2010, pages II and III.
12. Préfecture de la Réunion, *Annuaire de la coopération régionale à la Réunion*, 2010, p. 179.
13. Préfecture de Mayotte, *Annuaire de la coopération régionale à Mayotte*, 2010, p. 32.
14. Maldives, which have demonstrated some interest for the Indian Ocean Commission, is participating in the Indian Ocean Islands Games.

15. Oraison, "Cogestion de Tromelin : un accord critiqué", Témoignages, 14 June 2010.
16. Cointat, Rapport d'information sur les îles Éparses, Sénat (No. 299), Paris, p. 12.
17. This new name was proposed some years ago by Wilfrid Bertile, former Secretary General of the Indian Ocean Commission. The proposition has been made again in the context of *Les états généraux de l'outre-mer* held by France in 2009, and is presently making its way around the IOC circle and seems to be supported by all the COI members.
18. CEN-SAD, COMESA, EAC, ECCAS, ECOWAS, IGAD, SADC, and UMA. The IOC is not considered as a regional economic commission while the economic integration of its members is to be realised through COMESA and the future tripartite COMESA-EAC-SADC free-trade agreement.
19. European Community (2008), *Regional Strategy Paper and Regional Indicative Programme 2008-2013*, p. 21.
20. Treaty establishing the African Economic Community, Abuja (Nigeria), 3 June 1991.
21. Economic Partnership Agreements are the trade and development agreements that will replace the trade chapters of the 2000 Cotonou Agreement between the EU and the ACP countries. The exception of these chapters from WTO law expired in 2008, requiring both parties to put in place a WTO-compatible alternative. The European Union has committed to ensuring that the EPAs will guarantee both the development focus and the preferential trading terms currently enjoyed by ACP countries, while complying with WTO obligations. (source: European Community, 2006, "EU and Eastern and Southern Africa close first phase of Economic Partnership Agreement negotiations", EC06-043EN).
22. A Regional Indicative Programme represents the programmed European Union's financial aid in favour of a specific ACP region for a specific period of six years. In the ESA-IO Region, the Regional Indicative Programme assists Eastern and Southern Africa's regional organisations (COMEASE, EAC, IOC, and SADC) in meeting the challenges of implementing their medium-term strategies, which focus on establishing customs unions and moving to common markets and monetary unions in order to increase equitable prosperity across the whole region. (source: European Community, "*EC and the Region of ESA-IO. Regional Strategy Paper and Regional Indicative Programme 2008-2013*", p. 43).
23. Idem, p. 44.
24. Not taking into account Egypt and Libya that are COMESA members but part of the North Africa Region and the EUROMED Partnership.
25. Calculations made with data from CIA, *The World Factbook*, https://www.cia.gov/library/publications/the-world-factbook/, accessed 12 April 2011.
26. The Nairobi Convention (1995) provides a regional legal framework and coordinates the efforts of the member states to plan and develop programmes that strengthen their capacity to protect, manage and develop their coastal and marine environment sustainably. It also provides a forum for inter-governmental discussions that lead to better understanding of regional environmental problems and the strategies needed to address them; and promotes sharing of information and experiences in the WIO region and with the rest of the world. (source: Nairobi

Convention, "About", http://www.unep.org/NairobiConvention/about/index.asp, accessed on 13 April 2011)

27. The main objective of the Commission is to promote the sustainable utilisation of the living marine resources of the South-West Indian Ocean region, by the proper management and development of the living marine resources, without prejudice to the sovereign rights of coastal states and to address common problems of fisheries management and development faced by the Members of the Commission. The Commission has due regard for and promotes the application of the provisions of the FAO Code of Conduct on Responsible Fisheries, including the precautionary approach and the ecosystem approach to fisheries management (source: SWIOFC, "Regional Fishery Bodies Summary Descriptions: SWIOFC", http://www.fao.org/fishery/rfb/swiofc/en, accessed on 13 April 2011).
28. SWIOFP is an ambitious multinational research project with an overall goal that will see the West Indian Ocean's marine resources ecologically managed for sustainable use at the benefit of the region's riparian countries. The project forms part of the Large Marine Ecosystem Programme approach (LME) and is supported by the Global Environment Facility (GEF) as a contribution to its international waters programme and implemented by the World Bank. (source: SWIOFP, "Homepage", http://www.swiofp.net/, accessed on 13 April 2011).
29. The goal of the project is to ensure the long-term sustainability of the living resources of the ASCLME region by introducing an ecosystem-based approach to management. The overall project objectives are: (1) To acquire sufficient baseline data to support an ecosystem-based approach to the management of the Agulhas and Somali Current LMEs; and (2) To produce a Trans-boundary Diagnostic Analysis (TDA) and Strategic Action Plan (SAP) for both the Agulhas Current and Somali Current LMEs. (source: ASCLME, "The ASCLME Project", http://www.asclme.org/asclme_project/asclme_project.html, accessed on 13 April 2011)
30. ReCoMaP is a regional programme for the sustainable management of the coastal zones of the countries of the Indian Ocean. It is an initiative of the Indian Ocean Commission, funded by the European Union for a total of 18 million Euros. (source: ReCoMaP, "Homepage", http://www.recomap-io.org/, accessed on 13 April 2011)
31. The broad goal of the project was to address the degradation of the marine and coastal environment due to land-based activities in countries bordering the Western Indian Ocean (WIO). Its two major products have been: (1) the Protocol for the Protection of the Marine and Coastal Environment of the Western Indian Ocean from Land-Based Sources and Activities (LBSA Protocol) which was adopted on adopted on 31 March 2010; and (2) the Strategic Action Programme (SAP) for the Protection of the Western Indian Ocean from Land-Based Sources and Activities which was endorsed on 31 March 2010. (source: WIO-Lab, "Homepage", http://www.wiolab.org/, accessed on 13 April 2011)
32. The Mascarene Islands (Réunion, Mauritius, Rodrigues) and the Comoros Islands (including Mayotte) are purely oceanic in nature as they are hot spot volcanic islands and, therefore, are not really African in geological terms.
33. The EU has seven regions that are geographically very distant from the European continent but that still form an integral part of the EU member countries they belong to. Known as the "outermost regions", they are covered by EU law and

the other rights and duties associated with EU membership - in contrast to overseas territories, which have a different legal status. However, in the Treaty on the Functioning of the European Union, the outermost regions are covered by Article 349, which recognizes that EU policies must be adjusted to their special circumstances. (source: European Commission, "Regional policy – Europe's remotest regions", http://ec.europa.eu/regional_policy/themes/outermost/index_en.htm, accessed on 21 April 2011)

34. The IOR-ARC was formally launched at the first Ministerial Meeting in Mauritius on 6-7 March 1997. This meeting adopted the IOR-ARC Charter, and determined a number of administrative and procedural matters. The IOR-ARC combines officials, business and academics as an integral part of its functioning in a unique tripartite structure. It involves a co-ordinated endeavour of officials (CSO), academics (IORAG), and businesspeople (IORBF) of the member countries, ensuring that officials alone will not be responsible for its functioning. (source: DFA-RSA, "Indian Ocean Rim Association for Regional Cooperation (IOR-ARC)", http://www.dfa.gov.za/foreign/Multilateral/inter/iorarc.htm, accessed on 16 April 2011)
35. The Indian Ocean Tuna Commission (IOTC) is an inter-governmental organisation established under Article XIV of the FAO constitution. The objective of the commission is to promote cooperation among its members with a view to ensuring, through appropriate management, the conservation and optimum utilisation of stocks tuna and tuna-like species in the Indian Ocean, and encouraging sustainable development of fisheries based on such stocks. (source: IOTC, "About IOTC > mission", http://www.iotc.org/English/info/mission.php, accessed on 16 April 2011)
36. At present the Arusha Agreement of 1990 on the Organisation for Indian Ocean Marine Affairs Cooperation has been signed by nine countries (Indonesia, Iran, Kenya, Mauritius, Mozambique, Nepal, Pakistan, Sri Lanka, and Tanzania) and ratified by five (Indonesia, Mauritius, Mozambique, Pakistan, and Sri Lanka). Eight ratifications are needed for the Agreement to come into force. In the meantime, the IOMAC Technical Cooperation Group has begun to be activated following the Arusha Resolution, and a number of IOMAC activities have been implemented in the 1990s. Today, following the return to political normalcy in Sri Lanka, IOMAC is building up once more under the leadership of its Sri Lankan Secretary General Dr. Hiran W. Jayewardene.
37. The 'Indian Ocean Naval Symposium' (IONS) is a voluntary initiative that seeks to increase maritime cooperation among navies of the littoral states of the Indian Ocean region by providing an open and inclusive forum for discussion of regionally relevant maritime security issues and, in the process, endeavours to generate a flow of information between naval professionals that would lead to common understanding and possibly agreements on the way ahead. (source: Indian Navy, "Indian Ocean Navy Symposium", http://indiannavy.nic.in/ions_31jul10.pdf, accessed on 16 April 2011)
38. IOGOOS is an Association of marine operational and research agencies in the Indian Ocean Region. 27 organisations from 13 countries have become Members of IOGOOS and agreed to collaborate and work together for the implementation

of GOOS in the Indian Ocean and for promoting activities of common interest for the development of operational oceanography in the Indian Ocean region. (source: IOGOOS, "Homepage", http://www.incois.gov.in/Incois/iogoos/home.jsp, accessed on 16 April 2011)

REFERENCES

African Union Commission (2004), *Strategic Plan of the African Union Commission, Volume 1: Vision and Mission of the African Union*, Addis Ababa: African Union, p. 62.

ASCLME (online), Agulhas and Somali Current Large Marine Ecosystems Project, http://www.asclme.org/asclme_project/asclme_project.html, accessed on 13 April 2011.

Bertile, W. (2010), "Dans l'océan Indien, la richesse de l'intégration", *Le Monde Diplomatique*, March 2010, pages II and III.

Bouchard C. (2007), "France and United Kingdom as the 37th and 38th Indian Ocean Coastal States", *Indian Ocean Survey* (Indian Ocean Research Group), vol. 3, no. 1-2, pp. 36-52.

CIA – Central Intelligence Agency, "The World Factbook", https://www.cia.gov/library/publications/the-world-factbook/, accessed 3 April 2011.

Cointat, C. (2010), *Rapport d'information sur les îles Éparses*, Sénat (No. 299), Paris, p. 105.

CSO (2009), *Mauritius in Figures 2009*, Port Louis: Ministry of Finance and Economic Development, Central Statistics Office, p. 44.

DFA-RSA (online), "Indian Ocean Rim Association for Regional Cooperation (IOR-ARC)", Department of Foreign Affairs, Republic of South Africa, http://www.dfa.gov.za/foreign/Multilateral/inter/iorarc.htm, accessed on 16 April 2011.

European Community (2006), "EU and Eastern and Southern Africa close first phase of Economic Partnership Agreement negotiations", EC06-043EN (9/2/2006).

European Community (2008), *European Community and the Region of Eastern and Southern Africa and the Indian Ocean. Regional Strategy Paper and Regional Indicative Programme 2008-2013*, p. 53 + 17 annexes.

European Commission (online), "Regional policy – Europe's remotest regions", http://ec.europa.eu/regional_policy/themes/outermost/index_en.htm, accessed on 21 April 2011.

IEDOM (2010a), *Mayotte, Rapport annuel 2009*, Paris: Institut d'Émission des Départements d'Outre-Mer, p. 186.

IEDOM (2010b), *La Réunion, Rapport annuel 2009*, Paris: Institut d'Émission des Départements d'Outre-Mer, p. 206.

Indian Navy (online), "Indian Ocean Navy Symposium", http://indiannavy.nic.in/ions_31jul10.pdf, accessed on 16 April 2011.

INSEE-Réunion (2010), Tableau économique de La Réunion – Édition 2010. Saint-Denis: Institut national de la statistique et des études économiques, Direction régionale de La Réunion, p. 240.

IOC (online), "Indian Ocean Commission", http://www.coi-ioc.org/, accessed on 10 April 2011.

IOGOOS (online), "Indian Ocean Global Ocean Observing System", http://www.incois.gov.in/Incois/iogoos/home.jsp, accessed on 16 April, 2011.

IOTC (online), "Indian Ocean Tuna Commission", http://www.iotc.org/English/info/mission.php, accessed on 16 April 2011.

ITC - International Trade Centre, "Trade Map: trade statistics for international business development", http://www.trademap.org/, accessed on 3 April 2011.

MRD (2006), *National Action Programme of Adaptation to Climate Change*. Comoros: Ministry of Rural Development, Fisheries, Handicraft and Environment, p. 91.

Nairobi Convention (online), "Nairobi Convention", http://www.unep.org/NairobiConvention/index.asp, accessed on 13 April 2011.

NSB (2008), *Statistical Abstract 2007*. Victoria: Republic of Seychelles, National Statistics Bureau, p. 150.

Oraison, A. (2010), "Cogestion de Tromelin : un accord critiqué", *Témoignages*, June 14, 2010, http://www.temoignages.re/cogestion-de-tromelin-un-accord,43938.html, accessed on 10 April 2011.

Préfecture de la Réunion (2010), *Annuaire de la coopération régionale à la Réunion* (4th edition, update of December 2010), Saint-Denis (Réunion), p. 214.

Préfecture de Mayotte (2010), *Annuaire de la coopération régionale à Mayotte* (1st edition, June 2010), Mamoudzou (Mayotte), p. 32.

ReCoMaP (online), "Regional Coastal Management Programme", http://www.recomap-io.org/, accessed on 13 April 2011.

RTO – Rodrigues Tourism Office, "General Info", http://www.tourism-rodrigues.mu/index.php?p=220610125847, accessed 2 April 2011.

SWIOFC (online), "Southwest Indian Ocean Fisheries Commission", http://www.fao.org/fishery/rfb/swiofc/en, accessed on 13 April 2011.

SWIOFP (online), "Southwest Indian Ocean Fisheries Project", http://www.swiofp.net/, accessed on 13 April 2011.

UNDP (2010), *Human Development Report 2010 – 20th Anniversary Edition, The Real Wealth of Nations: Pathways to Human Development*. New York: United Nations Development Programme, p. 227.

UNDESA (2009), "Data (on-line)", *The 2008 Revision of the World Population Prospects*, New York: United Nations, Department of Social and Economic Affairs, Population Division, http://esa.un.org/unpd/wpp2008/index.htm, accessed 9 March 2011.

WIO-LaB (online), "Project Addressing Land-Based Activities in the Western Indian Ocean", http://www.wiolab.org/, accessed on 13 April 2011.

WRI - World Resources Institute, "Coastal and Marine Ecosystems: Country Profiles", Earth trends: the environmental portal. http://earthtrends.wri.org/country_profiles/index.php?theme=1, accessed 3 April 2011.

APPENDIX A

Basic Data for the South-West Indian Ocean Islands

	COM	MAD	MAU	MAY	RUN	Sc. Is [(a)]	SEY
Land area (sq km)	2,235	587,041	2,030	374	2,513	44	455
Geology	Volcanic	Continental	Volcanic	Volcanic	Volcanic	Sand/ coral	Granitic or Sand/coral
Highest point (m)	2,360	2,876	828	660	3,069	24	905
Coastline (km)	340	4,828	177	185	207	120	491
TS + EEZ (sq km)[(b)]	174,677	1,204,610	1,291,478	64,000	315,659	640,400	1,334,054
Population (mid-2011)	794,683	21,926,221	1,303,717	209,530	848,000 [(c)]	—	89,188
Pop. density (inh./sq km)	356	37	642	560	337	—	196
Pop. annual growth rate (%)	2.7	3.0	0.7	1.5	1.3 [(c)]	—	0.9
Median age (yrs)	19.0	18.2	32.7	16.7	31.5 [(c)]	—	32.5
Life expectancy at birth (yrs)	64.2	63.6	74.5	76.8	78.0 [(c)]	—	73.5
GNI in PPP per capita 2008 (US$)	1,176	953	13,344	8,000 [(c)]	22,800 [(c)]	—	19,128
HDI – 2010	0.428	0.435	0.701	0.690 [(c)]	0.800 [(c)]	—	0.730 [(c)]
GDP in PPP (billion US$)	0.789	20.730	17.490	1.800 [(d)]	20.000 [(d)]	—	1.908
Exports (millions US$)	32	1,096	1,769	7	308 [(d)]	—	397
Imports (millions US$)	195	3,159	3,729	502	5,221 [(d)]	—	853
Trade balance (millions US$)	-163	-2,063	-1,960	-495	-4,913 [(d)]	—	-456

TS: territorial sea. EEZ: exclusive economic zone. GNI in PPP: Gross national income in purchasing power parity (US$). HDI: Human Development Index. GDP in PPP: Gross domestic product in purchasing power parity (US$). (a) No permanent population. (b) Estimations. (c) Estimations based on available data (INSEE, IEDOM, PRB, UNDP). (d) Estimations based on data from IEDOM (2010a and 2010b).

Sources: CIA, *The World Factbook 2010* (land area, highest point, and coastline, population, growth rate, median age, and life expectancy, GDP in PPP); WRI, *Earth trends: the environmental portal* (territorial sea and claimed exclusive economic zone in 2000, referring to the Global Maritime Boundaries Database (GMBD); TAAF official website for the Scattered Islands; UNDP, *Human Development Report 2010* (GNI in PPP per capita, Human Development Index); ITC, *Trade Map: trade statistics for international business development* (imports and exports); IEDOM, *La Réunion, rapport annuel 2009* (for Réunion's economic data).

APPENDIX B

Abbreviations

ACP	Africa, Caribbean and Pacific
AfDB	African Development Bank
AIMS	Africa, Indian Ocean, Mediterranean, and South China Sea
AMF	Arab Monetary Fund
AOSIS	Alliance of Small Island States
ASEAN	Association of Southeast Asian Nations
ASLME	Agulhas and Somali Current Large Marine Ecosystems
AU	African Union
BIOT	British Indian Ocean Territory
CAF	Confederation of the African Football
CMMR	Comoros, Madagascar, Mauritius and Seychelles
COMESA	Common Market for Eastern and Southern Africa
EAC	East African Community
EEZ	Exclusive Economic Zone
EPA	Economic Partnership Agreement
ESA	Eastern and Southern Africa
ESA-IO	Eastern and Southern Africa and the Indian Ocean
EU	European Union
FTA	Free Trade Agreement
G77	Group of 77
HDI	Human Development Index
IBRD	International Bank for Reconstruction and Development (World Bank)
ICP	International Cooperating Partner (with SADC)
IDB	Islamic Development Bank
IFAD	International Fund for Agricultural Development
IFIOR	International Forum on the Indian Ocean Region
IGAD	Inter-Government Authority on Development
IGO	Intergovernmental Organisation
IMF	International Monetary Fund
IOC	Indian Ocean Commission (Commission de l'Océan Indien – COI)

IOGOOS	Indian Ocean Global Ocean Observing System
IOMAC	Indian Ocean Marine Affairs Cooperation
IONS	Indian Ocean Naval Symposium
IOR-ARC	Indian Ocean Rim-Association for Regional Cooperation
IORG	Indian Ocean Research Group
IOTC	Indian Ocean Tuna Commission
IOTO	Indian Ocean Tourism Organisation
IOZP	Indian Ocean Zone of Peace
LAS	League of Arab States
LDC	Least Developed Countries
NAM	Non-Aligned Movement
NGO	Non-governmental Organisation
OIC	Organisation of the Islamic Conference
OIF	International Organisation of La Francophonie (Organisation internationale de la francophonie – OIF)
REC	Regional Economic Commission
ReCoMaP	Regional Coastal Management Programme
RIP	Regional Indicative Programme
RIFF	Regional Integration Facilitation Forum
RO	Regional Organisation
SACU	Southern Africa Customs Union
SADC	Southern African Development Community
SAARC	South Asian Association for Regional Cooperation
SIDS	Small Island Developing States
SWIO	South-West Indian Ocean
SWIOFC	Southwest Indian Ocean Fisheries Commission
SWIOFP	Southwest Indian Ocean Fisheries Project
UN	United Nations
TAAF	Southern and Antarctic Lands
WIO-LaB	Addressing land-based Activities in the Western Indian Ocean
WTO	World Trade Organisation
WWF	World Wide Fund For Nature

Chapter 4
South Africa and the IOR-ARC: Shifting Priorities

Ruchita Beri

Introduction

Indian Ocean oft referred, as *al bahr Al Hindi* in the Arab navigational treaties has been a highway of commerce since the early civilisations.[1] The Indian Ocean Rim is a conglomeration of diverse countries, each with different community, different economic background and different per capita income. Economically, the region has small countries such as Seychelles with a population of less than 90,000 as compared to India's, which is over one billion. Geographically, the Indian Ocean is the third largest ocean of the world. It extends more than 75 million square kilometers and is about half the size of the Pacific and only smaller than the Atlantic. Further, while the other two oceans are open ended, in case of Indian Ocean, the Indian subcontinent brings the two opposing coasts together. Strategically, Indian Ocean is the main trading and transport connection in the world.[2] The resources of the Indian Ocean are vast – oil and gas, minerals, fish and other marine products. Two thirds of the world's oil resources are concentrated in the region, besides 40 per cent of the deposits of gold, 90 per cent of diamond and 60 per cent of uranium. Indian Ocean is also important from the sea-lines of communication (SLOC) point of view. From an environmental point of view, the Indian Ocean is of paramount importance with the requirement to protect the rare flora and fauna as also the forests with their complex bio-spherical relationships.

This paper examines South Africa's policy towards the Indian Ocean Rim Association for Regional Cooperation (IOR-ARC). In the mid-nineties the process of cooperation among the Indian Ocean Rim (IOR) countries was led by South Africa, India and Australia. This process led to the formation of IOR-ARC in 1997. South Africa's role in this tripartite endeavour was crucial because the concept of an IOR initiative was first mooted by South African Foreign Minister Pik Botha in November 1993. After the demise of apartheid regime and its return to the international fold, the IOR process provided a platform for Pretoria to hone its diplomatic skills and play a leadership role in this regional process. This chapter argues that various factors, the domestic debate and South Africa's preoccupation with emerging foreign policy concerns have refocused its attention away from IOR-ARC.

Evolution of IOR-ARC

The idea of cooperation between the Indian Ocean states can be traced back to Pandit Jawaharlal Nehru, India's first Prime Minister. He is on record discussed the commonality of the people's of the region and other leaders have acknowledged it. It was part of his vision of Afro- Asian unity. However, the advent of the Cold War, which led to the super power rivalry in the region, and also the apartheid regime in South Africa, hampered his vision from being implemented. Although, until the emergence of IOR-ARC there was no rim-wide institutional arrangement for cooperation in the Indian Ocean region, there have been a number of regional organisations in several parts of it. These are the Association of the South-East Asian Nations (ASEAN), the Gulf Cooperative Council (GCC), the Indian Ocean Commission (IOC), the South Asian Association for Regional Cooperation (SAARC), the Southern African Development Community (SADC) and the Indian Ocean Marine Affairs Cooperation Council (IOMAC).

The end of Cold War brightened the chances of cooperation in the rim. Previous efforts at creating unity had failed because of Cold War ideological differences. With these out of way the concept at last had a real chance. Further the establishment of the World Trade Organisation (WTO) to replace the GATT on 1 January 1995 gave new impetus to the process of global trade liberalisation and free trade. It also had implications for regional organisations. There were fears that regional groupings like the European Union (EU), Northern African Free Trade Agreement (NAFTA) and Asia Pacific Economic Cooperation (APEC) may become exclusive trading blocs. Thus the Indian Ocean may have been activated by this general trend towards regionalism as well as fear of exclusion from other regional groupings resulting in global marginalisation. It is believed that the IOR-ARC could act as a collective bargaining tool to enable the members to obtain more favourable trade agreements with these other groupings. Finally the emergence of new democratic South Africa after the 1994 elections, free from the shackles of apartheid hastened the process of the IOR-ARC.

The first step towards formation of IOR-ARC was taken by South Africa. During a visit to India in November 1993, South African Foreign Minister Pik Botha mooted the concept of an IOR-ARC. He identified IOR as an area of great mutual importance for both India and South Africa. In January 1995, President Mandela rekindled the prospect of such an initiative during a visit to India. He expressed that the growing business ties between South Africa and India could help shape a trading block among Indian Ocean Rim Countries. The South African president stated:

> "The natural urge of facts of history and geography that Nehru spoke of should broaden itself to include exploring the concept of an Indian Ocean Rim for socio-economic cooperation and improve the lot of the developing nations in multilateral institutions such as the United Nations, Commonwealth and the Non- aligned Movement".[3]

This proposal was enthusiastically received and culminated in an inter-governmental meeting that was held on 29-31 March 1995 in Port Louis in Mauritius. This meeting involved the core group of seven IOR countries (M-7) – Australia, India, Kenya, Mauritius, Oman, Singapore and South Africa. Accordingly, a Working Group of M-7 was set up to outline the principles and objectives, scope of activities and Work Programme. After two years of hectic interaction that involved three meetings of the working group and two IGMs, the IOR-ARC was formerly launched at the Ministerial meeting held in Mauritius from 5-7 March 1997. The fourteen founding members were – Australia, India, Indonesia, Kenya, Madagascar, Malaysia, Mauritius, Mozambique, Oman, Singapore, South Africa, Sri Lanka, Tanzania and Yemen. The Charter adopted at the meeting identifies the scope and objectives of the regional grouping and the focus is on economic cooperation in the region.[4] At present, there are 18 members of the organisation and four dialogue partners – Egypt, Japan, China and UK.[5]

South Africa and IOR-ARC: Initial Debate

The idea of an Indian Ocean Rim (IOR) regional bloc and South Africa's participation in it has been topic of hot debate ever since the dawn of the new 'rainbow' nation. However critics of the concept of IOR-ARC in South Africa argued about a number of conceptual problems with IOR and dilution of South Africa's commitment to Southern Africa.

The primary problem, the critics of IOR say, lies in its definition.[6] There are problems in identifying countries that are part of the IOR partly due to the size of the Indian Ocean. States surrounding the Indian Ocean have little in common with one another, and their everyday dealings on the international front are usually limited to their immediate neighbours. In view of some area regarded as the IOR represents an "unnatural, concocted rather than genuine regional arrangement. At best it comprises some sub-regional arrangements, i.e. Southern Africa, the Horn of Africa, the Middle East, South Asia, Southeast Asia and Australasia".[7] The objection to the size of the region can be easily ruled out. The Pacific Ocean is larger than Indian Ocean and yet there is an Asia-Pacific Organisation (APEC).

It has been argued that IOR concept was inspired by South Africa partly with a view to joining the "winning" nations of the East. However, it is felt that the existing foreign policy void of the government has allowed this concept to develop a "momentum of its own without an adequate elaboration of its rationale". Consequently, it is felt that South Africa has been reduced to following initiatives of others rather than shaping developments.[8]

Another obstacle viewed in the development of the Indian Ocean Rim formation is that trade flows among the countries littoral to Indian Ocean are very low, Using 1992 figures, trade flows among the "Core Countries" constituted a paltry 2.5 per cent of their total trade. If all the countries bordering the Ocean are considered, intra-trade flows amount to 9.2 per cent of total trade. Similarly, there is a low level of investment dependency among the participating countries. Much of the investment comes from countries outside the region. Though economic blocs have been created despite low levels of intra-regional trade and investment flows, the cardinal considerations have been economic interdependence, geographic proximity and close political affinities. The IOR seems to be weak on all these counts.[9]

Within South Africa, there is a strong political commitment to Southern Africa, notably to cooperation within Southern African Development Community (SADC). Established in 1980 as the Southern African Development Co-ordination Conference (SADCC), SADC was formed to reduce the region's economic dependence on South Africa, by acting as a conduit and coordinating centre for international and investment rather than promoting integration. In post apartheid era, SADC's original rationale has now collapsed alongwith it much of the initial international goodwill towards it and funding of its aims. SADC has, therefore, reoriented its policy towards regional cooperation with the newly democratic South Africa whom it looks upon as its main source of investment. In the recent years, SADC has promoted the idea of cross border investment and trade and labour and capital flows.

Southern Africa certainly occupies a unique place in South African strategy. In the words of former Minister for Foreign Affairs (now, International Relations and Cooperation), Alfred Nzo, "In terms of our foreign policy, Africa is clearly to be a priority in the years ahead ... the promotion of the economic development of Southern African region is of paramount importance...".[10] Political stability in the region is essential to the success of democratic process in South Africa. This explains South Africa's commitment to SADC and SACU. Further in economic terms, Southern Africa contributes the latter's only export market that absorbs manufactures and capital goods rather than primary products. Thus, any alternative grouping would have to be entered very carefully to avoid spoiling the delicate economic relations in the region.[11] Moreover, the SADC countries fear that South Africa's membership of IOR-ARC might lessen the commitment of South Africa towards Southern Africa.

Despite all these problems, from the South African perspective the IOR initiative contains explicit advantages. Some analysts are of the view that the IOR-ARC could act as an agency for regional cooperation, which could initiate and manage a series of trade liberalisation measures, thus fulfilling the region's substantial potential by integrating it further with the global economy.[12]

An Indian Ocean Rim grouping would give both South Africa and Southern Africa a stronger political and economic basis for negotiations with main regional economic associations and with international agencies such as the World Bank, and the European Development Fund. Given the predominance of powerful trading blocs like the European Union (EU) and North American Free Trade Area (NAFTA), the only way for many developing countries in the South to avoid economic marginalisation is to seek membership of a powerful trading group. The IOR offers the potential for this and can be considered a crucial step towards South-South economic cooperation.[13] Moreover, as the Indian Ocean region was the only major geographic region with no substantial grouping in place, the IOR-ARC would fill the gap.[14]

From South African perspective, the IOR-ARC provides means for closer ties with India, both in economic and political terms. The need for stronger ties with India was strongly endorsed by the South Africa's Deputy President, Thabo Mbeki in 1997.[15] As far as foreign policy identity is considered, in the post apartheid period, within the South African foreign policy framework, the global South took a priority. Immense value was attached to the IOR-ARC as a vehicle for promoting South- South relations.[16]

Shifting Priorities

It has been over fourteen years since the IOR-ARC was formed. While the representatives of member states have met frequently, a general lack of enthusiasm and absence of anything significant is noticeable.[17] For the South African government, the region continues to be of growing importance. As Deputy Minister Sue van der Merwe, noted at the 2006 Ministerial meeting in Tehran:

> ...we are once again made aware of the enormous economic potential of the Indian Ocean Rim...the Indian ocean carries half of the world's container ships, one-third of the bulk cargo traffic and two-thirds of the world's oil shipments... (and) is also rich in resources, ranging from food, fisheries to precious minerals, from agricultural wealth to valuable human expertise...(representing) a population of close to two billion people, making it a massive market. The strategic value of the Indian Ocean Rim is therefore beyond doubt...[18]

Apart from the strategic value, the South African government perceives it as an important mechanism to achieve their development agenda. As Deputy Minister Aziz Pahad noted in 2007, "Today, despite all our efforts, the vast majority of our peoples still live below the poverty data line. The positive impact of globalisation has still not materialised in many of our countries. This is why we give importance to the IOR-ARC initiative".[19]

In recent years, Pretoria, in an attempt to re-energise the organisation has seconded an official to the secretariat at Mauritius and senior officials in the South Africa's Department of International Relations and Cooperation (DIRCO) are quite keen on IOR-ARC; nevertheless over the years a shift in priorities is noticeable.[20] First of all, building bridges with African neighbours has received priority over IOR-ARC. In that spirit, the South Africans wanted the members of the Southern African Development Community getting on board the IOR-ARC. However, that proposal has not worked.

Commitment to Africa

There is no doubt that Pretoria's commitment to IOR-ARC has been sidelined by its growing interest in the region. Of late, South Africa has listed its overarching foreign policy priorities as follows:[21]

(a) Continued prioritisation of the African continent;
(b) Strengthening political and economic integration of the SADC;
(c) Strengthening South-South relations;
(d) Strengthening relations with strategic formations of the North;
(e) Strengthening political and economic relations;
(f) Participate in the Global System of Governance.

South Africa's priority towards Africa crystallised with the Thabo Mbeki's call for African renaissance. In a statement addressed to the ANC on the occasion of the adoption of the new South African constitution, Mbeki famously declared "I am African", linking South Africa's destiny to that of the continent. One year later, he elaborated the concept and priority of an African renaissance, a rebirth to consist of among other things, the protection of human rights, peace, development, economic growth and establishment of stable and well governed democracies in Africa.[22] In Thabo Mbeki's words:

"An African renaissance must bring an end to these dictatorships, and to the civil wars that have given Africa the distinction of having the largest number of refugees in the world [...] We have to address the abuse of the notion of national sovereignty, where terrible things would be going on within the borders of a particular country while the rest of the country stands paralysed because taking action would be seen as interference".[23]

Apart from emphasising the need for economic and political renewal in the continent, Mbeki also underlined the need for transformation of global political and economic order. As Sidiropoulos reflects,"South Africa's vision is thus of a more equitable international system globally and an African renaissance".[24]

South Africa's vision of economic transformation of the continent found place in the New Partnership for Africa's Development (NEPAD) initiative, endorsed by the Organisation of African Unity (OAU) in 2001. The Mbeki government was instrumental in negotiating this initiative aimed at promoting economic and social development in the continent. The NEPAD identifies, amongst other things, democracy, governance, peace and security, economic and corporate governance, infrastructure and information technology, human resource development and market access as prerequisites for development.[25]

Emergence of IBSA

The IOR-ARC's importance has diminished to a certain extent with the creation of IBSA dialogue forum. Inaugurated in June 2003, the India-Brazil-South Africa (IBSA) Trilateral Dialogue Forum is a unique model of trans-national cooperation, as the three democratic countries represent three different continents and yet share similar worldviews and aspirations.

The areas identified for cooperation are diverse including agriculture, climate change, environment, education, energy, health, science and technology, tourism, trade, transport, culture and defence amongst others. The forum is not merely a grouping for South-South cooperation, but it is a strategic partnership between the three countries. Within IBSA, South Africa along with India and Brazil has pushed for global governance reform (such as the UN system and the WTO). In this regard South Africa's goals have been to "make the rules of global governance more fair and transparent".[26]

The emergence of IBSA Forum has further diluted the importance of IOR-ARC mechanism. South Africa's objectives to promote South-South cooperation aims at creating various forums for exchange among the leaders of South and the IBSA Forum provides that channel. At the same time, the IBSA forum has fulfilled South Africa's objective of developing closer ties with India. The South African President Zuma has reiterated the need to work towards South-South cooperation and at the beginning of June 2010, he paid his first presidential visit to an Asian country since taking office in May 2009. Emphasising the importance of South-South cooperation and a new 'look east' foreign policy, Zuma chose India as the country of choice to visit in order to strengthen bilateral and trade relations.

South Africa's Entry in BRICS

South Africa's entry into BRIC (Brazil, Russia, India, China and South Africa) cooperation mechanism may further decrease its interest in the IOR-ARC. Within South Africa, the media and experts have described South Africa's accession to BRICS an important milestone, indicative of South Africa becoming a major emerging economy in the world. It also reflects the growing magnitude of its strategic importance on the African continent. Prime motivation of South Africa's entry into BRICS is to speed up the country's economic development and also promote its African agenda.[27] From 2000 to 2008, BRIC trade with Africa has expanded seven times; hence from South Africa's perspective through BRICS, it will able to promote agenda's related to Africa on the international arena and promote South-South cooperation.

Conclusion

The formation of IOR-ARC triggered a debate within South Africa. The critics of the concept of IOR in South Africa highlighted the structural problems within IOR-ARC i.e. it covered a vast region, the membership was diverse both in terms of economies and political openness. Moreover, there were concerns that the membership of IOR-ARC would dilute South Africa's commitment to Southern Africa. Further it was also felt that due to lack of focus on this issue by the government, South Africa was reduced to following initiatives of others rather than shaping developments on the Indian Ocean region. The proponents of this initiative in South Africa were of the view that if security arrangements could be excluded and IOR confined itself to trade, the region had tremendous potential for loose intra-trade opportunities, opening markets, and developing entrepreneurial and business linkages.

However, over the years shifting priorities of the leadership and emergence of other regional groupings has led to decline in South Africa's interest in the IOR-ARC. During President Thabo Mbeki's administration, South Africa became more interested in dealing with issues related to the African region. Mbeki's active interest in the African renaissance kept him preoccupied in finding "African solutions for African problems". Thabo Mbeki, along with select African leaders, played a pivotal role in developing the 21st century version of African renaissance and in evolving the New Partnership for African Development. The African renaissance became the driving force turning IOR-ARC into a peripheral issue.

From South African perspective, one of the important objectives of joining the IOR-ARC was to develop closer ties with India. Formation of other groupings such as the India, Brazil and South Africa (IBSA) trilateral dialogue forum (2003) have provided an alternate platform for keeping India engaged. Finally, South Africa's decision to join BRIC (the Brazil, Russia, India and China), a grouping of emerging powers has diminished the relevance of IOR-ARC as an instrument to promote South-South cooperation and to articulate African interests.

END NOTES

1. Ashin Das Gupta and M.N. Pearson, Ed., *India and the Indian Ocean 1500-1800,* Calcutta: Oxford University Press, 1987, p. 9.
2. Government of India, India in the IOR-ARC: towards a new partnership in the Indian Ocean, March, 1997, p. 1.
3. President Nelson Mandela's address at the Rajiv Gandhi Foundation New Delhi, 25 January, 1995 *India Digest* (Pretoria), vol. 4, May 1996, p.10.
4. See *Resolution on the adoption of the charter of the Indian Ocean Rim- Association for regional cooperation,* First Ministerial Meeting, Mauritius, 5-7 March, 1997.
5. In 1999 the membership was expanded to include Iran, the UAE, Thailand and Bangladesh. Thus apart from India, IOR-ARC members include Australia, Bangladesh, Indonesia, Iran, Kenya, Madagascar, Malaysia, Mauritius, Mozambique, Seychelles, Singapore, South Africa, Sri Lanka, Tanzania, Thailand, United Arab Emirates and Yemen. See Mridula Krishna, "Indian minister in Oman for Indian Ocean Rim meet" at www.indiaabroaddaily.com See. Government of India, *India in the IOR-ARC: towards a new partnership in the Indian Ocean*, March, 1997.

6. There are number of works that deal with this issue of definition of the IOR. For a summary of these debates see Freer, G 'Problems in defining the Indian Ocean Region', *East Asia Project Working Paper Series* No.8, September 1995. Department of International Relations, University of Witwatersrand.
7. Mfundo C Nkuhlu, Department of Trade and Industry, in Chris Landsberg et al ed., *Mission Imperfect: Redirecting South Africa's Foreign Policy*, Center for Policy Studies, Johannesburg, 1995, p. 57.
8. See Landsberg et al, op.cit.
9. Mfundo C. Nkuhlu, "South Africa and the concept of the Indian Ocean Rim. A strategic political and economic analysis" in *South Africa and the Indian Ocean Rim: Obstacles and Opportunities,* FGD Occasional Paper No.4, January 1996, p. 16.
10. Statement by the Minister of Foreign Affairs, Alfred Nzo, to the parliamentary portfolio Committee on Foreign Affairs, 14 March 1995.
11. See Campbell & Scerii, op. cit, p. 25.
12. Conrad Strauss, "The Indian Ocean Rim: a South African Perspective", *SAIIA Review*, vol. 5, no. 2, October 1997, pp. 10-11.
13. Gwyn R. Campbell and Mario Scerii, "The prospects for an Indian Ocean Rim (IOR) Economic Association", *The South African Journal of International Affairs,* vol. 2, no. 2, Winter 1995, pp. 12-14.
14. Greg Mills, "South Africa and Security building in the Indian Ocean Rim" *Canberra Papers on Strategy and Defence,* no. 127, p. 100.
15. Ibid.
16. Ibid.
17. A non-paper circulated by the IOR-ARC secretariat in 2007, highlighted the problems within the organisation. Prominently it revealed, the delay among the core group members towards conceptualising the format of economic summit, delays and cancellation of meetings, lack of funds and technical staff at the secretariat.
18. Statement delivered by South Africa's Deputy Minister for Foreign Affairs, Sue van der Merwe, at the General Debate during the Sixth meeting of the Council of Ministers of the Indian Ocean Association for Regional Cooperation at http://www.dfa.gov.za/docs/speeches/2006/merw0221.htm as accessed on 10 April 2011.
19. Statement by Deputy Minister Aziz Pahad at the General Debate during the Seventh meeting of the Council of Ministers of Indian Ocean Association for Regional Cooperation at http://www.dfa.gov.za/docs/speeches/2007/paha0314.htm as accessed on 10 April 2011.
20. See, Statement by Deputy Minister Aziz Pahad, op cit. Also feed back from South African officials on this issue suggests an interest within the government on this issue. However during the last IOR-ARC officials meeting the South African representation was at a lower level, as the senior officials were involved in a BRICS meeting.
21. South Africa, Department of International Relations and Cooperation, *Strategic Plan 2010-2013.*
22. Eddy T Maloka, "The South African 'African renaissance' debate: a critique"

Africa Institute of South Africa at http://www.polis.sciencespobordeaux.fr/vol8ns/maloka.pdf accessed on 4 April 2011.

23. Elizabeth Sidiropoulos, "The foreign policy of South Africa" at http://www.ipri.pt/eventos/pdf/Artg%204_ES.pdf accessed on 2 April 2011.
24. Ibid.
25. Chris Landsberg, *South Africa's global strategy,* FES Briefing Paper 16, November 2006, p. 5.
26. Sidiripolous, op cit.
27. Francis Kornegay, "SA entry into BRIC revisited" at http://www.igd.org.za/coponent/content/article/61 accessed on 28 April 2011.

Chapter 5

IOR-ARC: Failures, Successes and Prospects

Saman Kelegama

Introduction

The Indian Ocean Rim Association for Regional Cooperation (IOR-ARC) is now fourteen years old. It is a regional grouping that came into operation with 14 countries in 1997 (Australia, Indonesia, India, Sri Lanka, Singapore, Malaysia, Oman, Yemen, Kenya, Tanzania, South Africa, Mozambique, Mauritius, and Madagascar) that later, in 1999, expanded to 19 countries (with Thailand, Bangladesh, Seychelles, United Arab Emirates, and Iran) and reduced to 18 countries in 2005 (Seychelles withdrew its membership in 2005). Five Dialogue Partners (Egypt, Japan, China, UK, and France) and one observer (Indian Ocean Tourism Organisation) constitute the others in the IOR-ARC.[1] The three key players in the IOR-ARC are Australia, India, and South Africa.

Its origins go back to the early 1990s when South Africa had just dismantled the apartheid regime and was trying to assert its identity and regional space. The South African Foreign Minister on a visit to India mooted the idea of an Indian Ocean regional grouping in late 1993. This was a time when India was not very happy with the progress of SAARC and its application for APEC membership was rejected and India had initiated a 'Look East' policy.[2] India also wanted to assert its position in a stronger regional grouping. In 1995, the Australian Foreign Minister had ideas of contesting for the UN Secretary-General's position and wanted political support for his candidature. This was also the time when Australia had initiated a 'Look West' policy and investigating

Australia's trade with South Asia.[3] The fusion of 'Look East' policy of India with Australia's 'Look West' policy together with South Africa's need for a regional identity and the politics of that time, resulted in the IOR-ARC in 1997. Frustration with slow progress in the existing regional groupings, fears of globalisation, and other factors may have driven some countries in the Indian Ocean rim to embrace IOR-ARC membership with enthusiasm at this stage.

It was an Association that wanted to emulate APEC from the very beginning. Thus, 'open regionalism' was embraced as its operational framework although it is not explicitly stated in the IOR-ARC Charter. Australia was the main proponent of this concept given its membership and leading role in the APEC. Open regionalism does not bind member countries by any commitments, it is based on voluntary action, and decisions are taken on the basis of consensus. The main areas for voluntary action are: trade liberalisation, and trade and investment facilitation. Sectoral cooperation projects also play a role in open regional arrangements under economic and technical cooperation (ecotech). However, unlike APEC where the heads of states preside over the annual meetings, IOR-ARC's key meetings are held only once in two years and are presided by the foreign ministers of the member states. It also does not have an active 'second track' (like the Pacific Economic Cooperation Council [PECC] in APEC) that acts like a 'think tank' to the 'first track'. A 'second track' that existed at the start of IOR-ARC in 1995 suffered a natural death by late 1997.[4] Unlike APEC, IOR-ARC also does not have a global or regional vision.[5]

The regional grouping functions on the premise that WTO-based liberalisation and global integration is too complicated, cumbersome, and unsympathetic towards some countries. Thus, operating regionally could improve the situation. In open regional arrangements, countries outside the regional grouping do not get affected. Thus, its main proponents consider the IOR-ARC functional framework of open regionalism as a building bloc of the WTO liberalisation agenda (see, for instance, Kelegama, 2000a).

IOR-ARC functions are based on a tripartite dialogue among Business Groups, Academic Groups, and Senior Officials. Based on these dialogues, suggestions on trade liberalisation, trade and investment facilitation and sectoral cooperation projects are fed to the Council of

Ministers to determine the policies of the regional groupings agenda. During the last fourteen years, the IORBF (Indian Ocean Rim Business Forum) and IORAG (Indian Ocean Rim Academic Group) have worked on a number of projects and completed reports for consideration by the Committee of Senior Officials (CSO) and thereafter the Council of Ministers.[6] The project coordination and other related administrative work is handled by the Secretariat of the IOR-ARC based in Mauritius. Despite fourteen years of operation, with six Ministerial meetings (1997 – Mauritius, 1999 – Mozambique, 2001 – Oman, 2003 – Sri Lanka, 2006 – Iran, and 2010 – Yemen), and twelve meetings of the CSO, IOPRBF, and IORAG (1997 and 1998 – Mauritius, 1999 and 2000 – Mozambique, 2001 and 2002 – Oman, 2003 and 2004 – Sri Lanka, 2006 and 2008 – Iran, 2009 and 2010 – Yemen), IOR-ARC has hardly anything to show as achievements. This situation needs examination.

This chapter highlights the failures, briefly sheds light on some of the achievements of the IOR-ARC, flags the emerging issues and explores future prospects for the regional association.

Failures of IOR-ARC

(a) Treatment of Least Developed Countries and Small Developing Countries

In a regional grouping, the least beneficiary member countries always feel that the increase of IRT through the regional arrangement should not increase the existing lop-sided situation. If a Preferential Trading Arrangement (PTA) was the governing framework of the regional arrangement, there are ways to assist less developed countries in a region by giving favoured rules of origin or preferential tariffs. This has been practised in many PTAs including ASEAN and SAARC is called "Special and Differential Treatment". In open regionalism, where voluntary action on trade liberalisation or trade and investment facilitation governs the operations, there are no preferences or additional measures for least developed member countries. Australia and Singapore are equal partners with Bangladesh and Mozambique for voluntary action. This gives a perception that the stronger countries are greater benefactors from uniform voluntary action. Thus, voluntary action by less developed countries is restricted due to this perception.

The point that needs emphasis is that the asymmetry between countries, in particular, the vastly different initial conditions has not been adequately addressed in the open regionalism framework used by the IOR-ARC. Australia, the main proponent of open regionalism in the IOR-ARC, seems to have totally over-estimated the willingness of member states to engage in voluntary action under these circumstances.

(b) Problems of the Free Rider and Lack of Reciprocity

Even in the APEC, where open regionalism has been practised for more than a decade, the Individual Action Plans (IAP) three-fourth based on voluntary action three-fourth of member countries have been far from satisfactory (ESCAP, 1998; Kelegama, 2000b; and others). This is because, non-members will obviously benefit by being 'free-riders' from trade, investment impediment removals and facilitation measures.

Dialogue partners, in particular, who will have more access to the details of the functioning of the regional grouping, will be key beneficiaries without any voluntary action. In any international transactions, reciprocity has become a key factor over the years and thus unilateral liberalisation in a grouping has become unrealistic from a political economy perspective, irrespective of theoretical merits.

(c) Open Regionalism Malfunctioning and Effective Sectoral Cooperation Taking Time

It was clear during the 1999 Ministerial meeting in Maputo, Mozambique that the core component of open regionalism is not operational in the IOR-ARC and that it is only partial open regionalism that could work in the IOR-ARC. In other words, Early Voluntary Sectoral Liberalisation (EVSL) like APEC is not workable in the absence of voluntary trade liberalisation in IOR-ARC. Australia's view was that under these circumstances, if one is to make sense of the open regionalism framework in the IOR-ARC, it should specifically focus on trade and investment facilitation issues. Since the projects undertaken by IORAG and IORBF belonged to various disciplines, Australia made the suggestion in 1999 that these projects should be streamlined and prioritised to be in line with trade and investment facilitation. All member countries accepted the suggestion. This led to the formation of a Working Group on Trade and Investment (WGTI) in January 2000, where the Group was requested to formulate an action plan to expedite trade and investment facilitation.

The WGTI delegated work on the preparation of a compendium on Customs Quarantine, etc., to various member countries. The streamlining of projects also became a priority item of the WGTI. Obviously, in this process, pet projects of Indian Ocean sub-regions were bound to become marginalised.

In fact, sectoral projects selected by the IORBF and IORAG were not appealing to all members. Some of them were based on sub-regional issues that were of little relevance to other countries. Some sectoral projects did not make much sense from the perspective of trade and investment facilitation. The experience of other regional groupings with sectoral cooperation is that they are time consuming (Kelegama, 1998).

(d) Expansion before Consolidation – Housekeeping Matters overriding Economic Action Matters

The problems were aggravated by the expansion of membership in 1999 before consolidation of the Association. In other words, widening took place before deepening the regional grouping. One wonders whether open regionalism was interpreted by member states as 'open for any member' as this definition is among the many other vague definitions of open regionalism by its main proponent Bergsten (1997).[7] In actual fact, IOR-ARC was confined to seven countries (Australia, India, South Africa, Mauritius, Kenya, Oman and Singapore) at the very beginning from 1995-1996, but later (1997) expanded to 14 to make it more representative of the Indian Ocean Rim. Many applicants thereafter were considered on a case-by-case basis, and as mentioned, in 1999, five more countries were included. The application of Pakistan for membership was rejected by the IOR-ARC as it does not offer MFN status to one of the IOR-ARC members, viz., India.

The politics of membership came into IOR-ARC before substantive issues were sorted out and integration was deepened. There was no moratorium for membership in late 1990s like in the APEC. When the membership increases in a regional grouping that functions according to consensus, it becomes difficult to manage and decision-making slows down. This happened to be the case in the IOR-ARC. The increase in membership also diverted the Association's energy for drafting rules and guidelines for its normal functioning; consequently, discussion of guidelines and procedures took precedence over discussing policy issues and economic integration action plans.

The membership increase has of course made IOR-ARC to boast as a regional grouping that accounts for half the world's population and controls a large reservoir of mineral resources. But such acclamations by IOR-ARC enthusiasts have no real validity in a practical sense in the modern day world.

(e) Multiplicity of RTA Membership

The other problem is that most IOR-ARC member countries are already members of other regional groupings like ASEAN, SAARC, GCC (Gulf Cooperation Council), SADEC (Southern Africa Development Cooperation), APEC, etc. Thus, they consider IOR-ARC as an addition and it does not receive the same priority as a closed regional grouping due to its wide geographical spread. Moreover, all the above-mentioned regional trading arrangements are binding and formal arrangement exists to drive trade unlike IOR-ARC which depends on a highly informal framework called open regionalism.

Previous studies have shown that intra-regional trade (IRT) among IOR-ARC countries to be close to 18-20 per cent (Kelegama, 1998; Kumar and Mohanthy, 2000; and others). Although it is quite high, this aggregate figure is deceptive because it does not reveal the spread of IRT. Disaggregate studies show that the two ASEAN members (viz., Singapore and Malaysia) account for the bulk of the trade in the region while intra-regional trade for Mauritius and Mozambique is high due to strong trading links with South Africa. IRT of Oman, Indonesia, South Africa, and Madagascar does not exceed 10 per cent (ACCI, 1998; Kelegama, 1998; Kumar & Mohanthy, 2000). In other words, the high IRT in IOR-ARC is due to heavy concentration of trade among some neighbouring countries, which is already covered by the existing regional trading arrangement members.

(f) Weak Role of the Secretariat

The IOR-ARC sectoral projects have to be effectively coordinated by the Secretariat. The manpower of the Secretariat counts and here the IOR-ARC record cannot be considered satisfactory.

The IOR-ARC Secretariat is located in Mauritius and remains a powerless body acting like a post office with a coordination role. It cannot drive the association between the ministerials or between the senior officials meetings. It was suggested that the Coordinating

Secretariat should be strengthened to ensure that the objectives of IOR-ARC are achieved. This was not to the liking of some member countries who felt that there was no necessity to create another bureaucracy.

This problem was further aggravated by inherent weakness of the tripartite dialogue. One problem of the tripartite dialogue is that its follow-up needs some degree of continuity in personnel involved. With frequent change of ministers and senior officials in individual member countries, certain project items go through a full circle of reviews over and over again thus consuming a considerable amount of time. Regime changes in individual IOR-ARC countries also contribute to the varying enthusiasm on IOR-ARC.[8]

(g) Vision not Acceptable

For those countries that supported IOR-ARC with an intention of getting more market access to member countries, there was a sudden bolt in late 1998. The Australian Chamber of Commerce and Industry aggressively campaigned for voluntary trade liberalisation and proposed 2020 as the target year for a free trade regime in the IOR-ARC (ACCI, 1998). This was quite similar to the 'Bogor targets' of APEC. The document with this proposal was submitted to the senior officials meeting in March 1998. There was no consensus on trade liberalisation. Thus, in December 1998, a meeting was summoned in Perth to discuss trade liberalisation agenda, but the topic was completely knocked-out from the IOR-ARC's agenda much to Australia's disappointment. Majority of the member states made it absolutely clear that they are not prepared to make departures from the WTO timetable of trade liberalisation. This was the time that Australia realised that APEC formulas like 'Bogor targets', IPA's are not workable in IOR-ARC and that Australia is dealing with a different kettle of fish.

In the 2001 Ministerial meeting in Oman, Sri Lanka suggested that IOR-ARC should have a vision and a clear idea of its future and thus suggested the formation of an Eminent Persons Group like in the APEC. After considerable deliberations, it was decided to form a High Level Task Force (HLTF) in 2001 to give a sense of direction to the IOR-ARC and assist the WGTI to streamline the projects. The HLTF Report is not a EPG type of Report giving a Vision for IOR-ARC, rather it is a report that gives some direction to strengthen trade and investment. Despite these attempts, the enthusiasm of the member countries, particularly, the powerful countries, seems to be waning away. One reason is that trade and investment strengthening is also based on voluntary action, which has miserably failed in the IOR-ARC in the last fourteen years.

At the Senior Officials meeting in May 2002 in Oman, Sri Lanka came up with an alternative proposal to make IOR-ARC a PTA. A PTA was vehemently opposed by Australia from the very beginning, but it came back to the agenda five years later. The argument is that open regionalism based on voluntary action has not worked in the IOR-ARC, thus to make the Association more result-oriented it has to have some bindings which the PTA could enforce. Sri Lanka came up with this proposition in order to give a face-lift to IOR-ARC and rescue it from natural disintegration.

Leaving aside the objection of some members, the idea of a PTA for IOR-ARC is not free from problems. Many IOR-ARC countries are already members of PTAs such as ASEAN, SAARC, GCC, SADEC, and so on. Thus, another PTA can give rise to a "spaghetti bowl" phenomenon (*a la* Bhagawati, 2002) with additional preferential tariffs, and rules of origin for customs to monitor and leading to a cumbersome situation. It has been argued that if some members are against a PTA, then it could be considered sub-regionally in the IOR-ARC. In fact, the PTA may have to be sub-regional in the IOR-ARC, because the GCC has been discussing formation of a Customs Union since 2003.[9] This will restrict Gulf member nations from joining a proposed IOR-ARC PTA due to their commitment to a common external tariff. It has been suggested that the PTA study should look into a two-track approach to a PTA – which will permit a sub-regional PTA to come into effect.

As some members were reluctant to go ahead with this idea, it was suggested that a 3 + X formula be used to form a PTA, i.e. if three members or more are willing to form a PTA then they should be allowed to go ahead to form a PTA. But this suggestion too was not seen positively given the fact that the members were already in PTAs, and they did not want to over-burden themselves by forming more PTAs. However, the PTA debate still goes on in IOR-ARC and a sub-committee is preparing another draft version of PTA for IOR-ARC. In short, IOR-ARC does not have a clear future pathway other than the proposed sectoral cooperation strategy.

(h) Falling Apart of the Second Track

Australia, a key player in the IOR-ARC, was one of the most enthusiastic members in the mid-1990s. This enthusiasm was reflected in its initiative to form a 'second track' via IFIOR (International Forum on Indian Ocean Rim) in June 1995 and initiating the ever-ambitious INDOTIP (Indian Ocean Trade and Investment Project) under its 'second track' focal point.

Australia's enthusiasm, however, waned after the second ministerial Conference in Maputo in 1999, when it realised that voluntary trade liberalisation would not take place, thus nullifying its immediate expectation from IOR-ARC, i.e. obtaining larger market access to member countries. By this time, INDOTIP had completely fallen apart. The Indian Ocean Centre in Perth ceased to function from 2000 due to cut-backs on funds from the new Australian government, that was elected in late 1995.

(i) Dwindling Interest

A senior Australian official headed the ministerial delegation to Muscat in 2001, Tehran in 2006 and Sanna in 2010, with the minister being absent. All these signs were a clear indication of the gradual losing of interest. Australia seems to be looking at medium-term market access via removal of barriers to trade and investment. A publication on IOR-ARC by the Australian Department of Foreign Affairs & Trade reflects this thinking (DFAT, 2000).

South Africa lost interest much earlier when around 1994 it became a member of SADEC. Rectifying past antagonisms and building bridges with African neighbours has received priority over IOR-ARC. Since Mbeki became President of South Africa, focus has been mostly on converting the Organisation of African Unity to an African Union and this objective is tied to the New Partnership for African Development initiated in 2001. The African renaissance has become the driving force for new partnerships and IOR-ARC has become a peripheral issue.

India still shows some interest, but is watching the situation. India was also not represented by the Foreign Minister since the 3rd Ministerial Conference in Oman. For India, IOR-ARC has not become a vehicle to assert its regional space as envisaged earlier. Neither has it become a major source of stimulating trade and investment. Its 'Look East' policy received a boost from receiving dialogue partner status in the ASEAN, proposed ASEAN-India FTA discussions, and JACIK (Japan, ASEAN, China, India and Korea) initiative. India is increasingly looking to USA and EU after its success in the area of IT and IOR-ARC has not excited India in recent years. Other member countries are also watching the situation. Some have become dormant – like Singapore, which sends junior delegations for most IOR-ARC meetings. IOR-ARC fatigue was visible in 2005 – Seychelles opted out of IOR-ARC while many other members expressed displeasure in the Association.

Given this scenario, Sri Lanka went out of the way to give some vigour to IOR-ARC when it held the Chair during 2003-05. At the 2003 Ministerial, Sri Lanka suggested that an annual Ministerial should be held instead of once in two years which was the practice before. This was supported by other members and accepted. Sri Lanka volunteered to appoint a new Executive Director to the IOR-ARC Coordinating Secretariat and this was done in 2004. At the 2004 Ministerial, Sri Lanka came up with a suggestion to develop an IOR-ARC Shipping Council, formulate an IOR-ARC Investment Protection Agreement, tourism cooperation with the Indian Ocean Tourism Organisation and share information and experience on the growing threat of international terrorism. The then Foreign Minister of Sri Lanka went to the extent of saying that if there is no purpose of IOR-ARC, it should be dissolved and 'one has to be frank about it'. However, all other members wanted to give IOR-ARC more time to mature and deliver.

Some Achievements

The very fact that IOR-ARC still exists after 14 years is an achievement. The formation of IOR-ARC has certainly improved networking among government/academic/business groups in the region. These contacts may have triggered additional trade and investment flows in the region which is not easily measurable.

The IORNET website (*www.iornet.com*) was created by FICCI, India, in order to provide possible business partners within the IOR-ARC with detailed economic and regulatory information on each IOR member country, covering fiscal and monetary scenarios, trade and investment policies and regulations; opportunities for trade, technology and investment tie-ups and practical guidelines for doing business in

IOR countries with addresses of key contacts in the respective governments and business organisations. This information may have led to business contacts.

It was proposed in 2002 that all IOR-ARC ministers and senior officials formally meet after the UN General Assembly meeting in New York in September every year. This was suggested to keep the regional grouping alive and ensure speedy follow-up action. The discussions in open regional groupings never tend to be focused on the economic agenda. While in the APEC the discussion gets diverted to East Timor (2000 Summit), Global Terrorism (2001 Summit), and other non-core topics, in IOR-ARC it is the logistical nitty gritties which take priority over deeper integration core issues. There is much talk but little action. One can only hope that the discussions will be on core issues.

Emerging Scenario

Why do members carry on with an unproductive organisation like IOR-ARC? The answer is straightforward i.e. once a nation becomes a member of such an organisation it feels obliged to participate irrespective of the outcome. The Bangkok Agreement (BA) that was formed in 1975 (India, Sri Lanka, Bangladesh, South Korea, and Laos) based on a 'positive list' approach PTA is a good example to illustrate this point. Despite poor achievements, it continued as a regional grouping with a number of meetings for over two decades. With the hope of giving some vigour, China was invited to become a member of the grouping in 2000 and the grouping was re-launched as the Asia Pacific Trade Arrangement (APTA) in 2005. Even though the two largest and fast growing economies in Asia (India and China) are now members of the APTA, still it remains a regional grouping that has as its governing framework a 'positive list' approach to tariff reduction. This has seriously acted as an impediment to exploit the potential of the grouping when the modern trend is to go for 'negative list' based regional PTA groupings.

The IOR-ARC will not attract a new dynamic member like the BA to invigorate it because currently there is no big regional player that can come in to do so. The process of sectoral cooperation consolidation in the IOR-ARC has not produced any results other than addressing mundane housekeeping and working structure issues.

A regional grouping purely based on economic integration without a political agenda (such as security) or a strong vision is difficult to sustain if there are no results from economic integration. This precisely happens to be the case in IOR-ARC. And why the economic integration is not functioning is because it is based on a vague concept called 'open regionalism' – what Prof. T. N. Srinviasan once called an oxymoron (Panagariya, 1999). Organisations based on voluntary action hardly move. Open regionalism has miserably failed to function and deliver so far wherever it has operated (Kelegama, 2000b).

The start of IOR-ARC had a number of flaws. Before working on substantive issues, IOR-ARC embarked on increasing membership and accommodating sectoral projects that had limited interest to some of the countries. Fusion of momentary factors brought nations around the Indian Ocean rim together and this regionalism was justified by historical factors, claiming that Indian Ocean merchants had a thriving network for trading at a time when monsoonal wind driven sailing vessels dominated the seas. Furthermore, in the mid-1990s regionalism was also viewed as a mechanism to face the threats of globalisation. The argument for this is weaker now. This is no longer the case, and many individual countries have got rid of the fears of globalisation. Looking for regional groupings to collectively address the threats of globalisation is no longer the case.

The view that EU took 50 years to progress and that IOR-ARC should have patience –as some commentators have argued – is no longer valid. In a globalised world, where the world is changing rapidly, regionalism has emerged to achieve quicker results – to 'fast track' liberalisation to gain more from trade and investment. If patience is what is needed, countries could very well follow the WTO timetable without taking the regional approach.

Consolidation of trade and investments agenda is not going to be easy. Trade and investment achievable initiatives have so far not been formed into an action plan. Also, to think that trade and investment facilitation based on voluntary action is going to move the Association is a myth. It is an Association that has shown to the world that the cost of cooperation can exceed the cost of non-cooperation. Sharing of ocean waters in the modern day world does not lead countries to be economically integrated. What can, for example, an Atlantic Ocean Rim

Association for Regional Cooperation deliver? In such a hypothetical regional grouping what will USA have in common with Angola? And what would Argentina have in common with Mauritania? The IOR-ARC is in a similar situation. The grouping is too diverse, geographically scattered with different levels of development in member countries for any meaningful integration to take place.

Prospects

Can anything be done to revive IOR-ARC? It has been informed that India will be taking up the IOR-ARC Chair with effect from 2011 and that Australia will be assuming the position of Vice-Chair. Both India and Australia being key players of IOR-ARC gives some hope for revival of the organisation. A few suggestions for revival could be made, but whether this will drive to enhance trade and investment flows in the region is questionable.

First, the IOR-ARC Charter should be revised to ensure deliverables. In other words, even without a PTA, ways and means should be explored to make some of the sectoral cooperation projects binding. For this purpose, the IOR-ARC should seriously consider setting up an Eminent Persons Group (EPG) and offer them a terms of reference (TOR) to come up with a vision and road map for IOR-ARC. The funding for the EPG could be mobilised via the IORBF and from member states. Second, India could propose to have IOR-ARC Summits from 2012 onwards with the heads of states meeting once in two years thereby giving more vigour and visibility to the Association. Third, IOR-ARC should make a concerted effort not to integrate with existing Indian Ocean Groupings such as Indian Ocean Marine Affairs Cooperation (IOMAC), Indian Ocean Tuna Commission (IOTC), Indian Ocean Naval Symposium (IONS), IOTO (Indian Ocean Tourism Organisation), IOZOP (Indian Ocean Zone of Peace) and the like, as they carry a lot of unwanted historical baggage and some of them happen to be pan-regional. The maximum accommodation could be as "observers" as has been the case with IOTO. Lastly, an effort must be made to reinvigorate the Second Track of the IOR-ARC which has fallen apart. Similar to PECC in APEC, IOR-ARC should promote a second track, which could be an effective "think tank" to the organisation. The newly formed Indian Ocean Research Group together with the Indian Council for

World Affairs could play a major role is establishing a new second track with the concurrence of the IOR-ARC Council of Ministers.

One can only hope that with such initiatives IOR-ARC could be given some vigour. Only time will tell how long IOR-ARC would last as a regional grouping.

END NOTES

1. Britain's interest in IOR-ARC is due to the fact that 13 Commonwealth countries are members of the IOR-ARC, while the interest of France is mainly due to its presence in the Indian Ocean through its territory of the Island of Reunion.
2. India became a Dialogue Partner of ASEAN in 1995.
3. Australia's Department of Foreign Affairs and Trade had completed a study in 1994 on Australia's trade relations with India titled "India's Economy at the Midnight Hour: Australia's India Strategy" and the Australia-South Asia Research Centre based at the Australian National University in Canberra initiated a study on Australia's economic relations with Sri Lanka titled "Cultivation of the Pearl", which was subsequently published by the Institute of Policy Studies in Sri Lanka in 1997.
4. Starting from the International Forum Indian Ocean Forum (IFIOR) in Perth in mid-1995, another two meetings of the second track took place in Delhi (December 1995) and Durban (January 1997). Thereafter the second track ceased to function.
5. For details, see Kelegama (1998 and 2000a).
6. These project proposals go through the CSO for comments and observations before going to the Council of Ministers.
7. For a critique of these definitions, see Kelegama (2000b).
8. For instance, the Liberal government of Australia does not attach the same importance as the Labour government did before 1995.
9. For details of the GCC, see, for instance, *The Economist*, 9-15th February, 2002: 43.

REFERENCES

Australian Chamber of Commerce and Industry (1998), "Working towards Complementarity – An Assessment of the Existing Multilateral and Regional Economic and Trade Policy Arrangements and Processes aimed at Identifying Opportunities for Trade and Investment Liberalisation within the Indian Ocean Rim Initiative", IORBF, Report submitted to the Senior Officials Meeting, Mauritius, March (referred to in the text as ACCI, 1998).

Bergsten, C.F. (1997), "Open Regionalism", *The World Economy*, vol. 20, no. 5, pp. 545-65.

Bhagwati, J. (2002), *Free Trade Today*, Oxford University Press, New Delhi.

DFAT (2000), *Enhancing the Trade and Investment Environment in the Indian Ocean Rim*, prepared by the Australia South Asia Research Centre, Australian National University for the Department of Foreign Affairs and Trade (DFAT), Canberra, Australia.

ESCAP (1998), *Implications of the APEC Process for Intraregional Trade and Investment Flows*, Studies in Trade and Investment, No. 33, Economic and Social Commission for Asia and Pacific, United Nations, New York.

Kelegama, S. (1998), "Can Open Regionalism Work in the Indian Ocean Rim Association for Regional Cooperation?", *ASEAN Economic Bulletin*, vol. 15, no. 2.

Kelegama, S. (2000a), "Open Regionalism in the Indian Ocean: How Relevant is the APEC Model for IOR-ARC?", *Journal of Asia Pacific Economy*, vol. 5, no. 3.

Kelegama, S. (2000b), "Open Regionalism and APEC: Rhetoric and Reality", *Economic and Political Weekly*, vol. XXXV, no. 51 (16 December).

Kumar, N. and S.K. Mohanty (2000), *Relevance of a Clearing and Payment Arrangement for the IOR-ARC Region*, RIS/IPS Publication, RIS, New Delhi.

Panagaria, A. (1999), "The Regionalism Debate: An Overview", *The World Economy*, vol. 22, no. 4, June.

Chapter 6
Refloating IOR-ARC: Australian Perspectives

Dennis Rumley

"*There once was an Ugly Duckling....*" or, The Sad History of the Good Ship IOR-ARC (McPherson, 2004)

A decade after its inception, the IOR-ARC appears to be dying a natural death (A South African official speaking in 2007 quoted in Gupta 2010, p. 61)

Australia's engagement with the countries of this region is now on the upswing (Rudd, 2010).

Introduction

Overall, it is clear that, with the 'collapse' of Cold War bipolarity, regionalism has become increasingly important in world politics, especially in the context of economic globalisation. Not surprisingly, since the end of the Cold War, there has been a resurgence of interest in regionalism among policy-makers, business people and academics. In many parts of the world, opportunities afforded by the end of the Cold War have resulted in a significant increase in regional institutionalisation.

The resultant proliferation in the number of regional groupings has led to a widespread debate over the causes and the effects of regionalism and the particular functions which regionalism might perform. In this context, we are especially interested in attempting to identify factors that lead to the success or failure of regionalism. As far as the Indian Ocean Rim Association for Regional Cooperation (IOR-ARC) is concerned, I am unaware of any academic, bureaucrat, businessperson or anyone else who would seriously argue that to date this regional grouping has been a resounding success. Indeed, there are few inhabitants around the Indian Ocean Region, including most Australians, who *have ever even heard* of the IOR-ARC acronym.

The principal purpose of the present paper is to discuss the changing motives which have led Australia to engage Indian Ocean states in lesser or greater degrees since the days of British colonial rule. More especially, my intention is to explore the geopolitics of why IOR-ARC has *not* been a resounding success from an Australian perspective, but, on a more positive note, what I also want to discuss is the rationale for a recent renewed interest in IOR-ARC by Australia.

It is a self-evident fact of geography that Australia is an Indian Ocean state. However, what I want to argue is that, from an Australian perspective, despite the creation of a 'Two Oceans' strategy, a 'Look West' policy and other political pronouncements, the combination of the internal structure of power within the Australian state and the geo-politics of Australia's regional relations have ensured that Australia's orientation to the Indian Ocean has only been able to be sustained in the short-term. Indeed, Australia's interest in Indian Ocean matters appears to have surfaced principally in response to external pressures and goals, and, in the post-Cold War period, generally on a ten-year cycle. Rather, Australia's geo-political imperatives have tended to push it towards the Pacific – *towards the north*, to east and Southeast Asia, and *towards the east* to the Pacific Islands and the United States. Any tendency to look 'West' was thus a euphemism for 'overlooking' the Indian Ocean and for reaffirming ties with Europe, especially Britain.

A set of mutual dependencies between Australia and states of the Asia-Pacific (narrowly-defined), the United States and Europe has generally contributed to a relatively weak set of Australian linkages with Indian Ocean states. Indian Ocean regionalism, therefore, from an Australian perspective, was always going to be accorded a lesser geo-political priority and links were thus going to remain underdeveloped. However, there are some recent signs that an Australian 'look west' policy is regaining prominence among strategic thinkers, politicians, businesspeople and others. This change is associated with a renewed interest in Indian Ocean regionalism, and thus in IOR-ARC, and is the result of a combination of changing national, regional and global geo-strategic and geo-economic circumstances. Overall, as the post-Cold War globalised, non-ideological world was in the process of re-configuring, it became increasingly preoccupied with new security challenges that in turn have had implications for the functioning and interests of the state. These challenges include the necessity for greater inter-state cooperation to enable environmental security, an increase in competition for energy security, the security of sea lanes of communication, the rise of India and China, and a range of other traditional and non-traditional security threats. In addition, from an Australian perspective, the rapid growth in India-Australia trade, the enduring strategic relationship with the United States and Australia's renewed interest in Africa are contributory factors to an increased interest in fostering a new regionalism among Indian Ocean states.

The 2009 Australian *Defence White Paper* argued that the Indian Ocean will have a much greater geostrategic significance in the period to 2030 and will join the Pacific Ocean in terms of its centrality to Australian defence planning and maritime strategy.[1] The changing strategic context in the Indian Ocean Region has caused one prominent commentator to suggest that the geo-political importance of Australia itself has fundamentally shifted from what he describes as a "strategic backwater" to a situation where Australia is now at "the southern tier of the focus of the global political system".[2]

Constructing and Deconstructing Regionalism

Since regionalism is 'constructed' and is not 'natural', then it is an inevitably contested concept both in theory and in practice. Competing views exist in terms of regional membership and regional goals, for example, as well as the particular emphasis which member states place upon these goals.

What is Regionalism?

Even a cursory examination of relevant social science literature reveals a multiplicity of definitions of the term regionalism. Secondly, depending on the point of view, regionalism can be seen to satisfy a wide range of social, economic, environmental and geopolitical functions. Regionalism can thus be conceptualised as being both informal and formal (or 'official'). It is informal in the sense that it can be equated with a sense of belonging or feeling of community in a socio-cultural sense – that is, it is a social construct associated with identity. From this perspective, regionalism can become a rationale for policies associated with stability and control within a perceived sphere of influence. This connects with an idealist view of community in which regional policies are designed to create regional benefits and that members receive an equitable share of those benefits.[3]

On the other hand, regionalism can be more formal or official. In this sense, it is created or constructed to meet certain state or other functions. As a result, there exist a variety of types of constructed regionalisms – economic, security and environmental. In a deterministic sense, geographical contiguity or propinquity has generally implied a degree of interest congruence between states. From this point of view, we can distinguish between three essential types of regionalism – first, *bilateral regionalism*, in which regional arrangements involve two contiguous states – for example, the Closer Economic Relations (CER) agreement between Australia and New Zealand; second, *trilateral regionalism*, in which the regional grouping comprises three contiguous states – for example, the numerous cases of 'growth triangles' designed principally for cooperative economic development at state peripheries; and third, *multilateral regionalism*, or regional arrangements involving several contiguous states and/or states adjacent to a regional of common concern, such as the Antarctic or the Indian Ocean. Regionalism is also not uni-scalar – that is, it can occur, be portrayed or be created at different scales. Thus, the contested regional concept, *Indian Ocean Region*, has been seen to be represented at a number of different scales – for example, the scale of an overarching Ocean Rim or Ocean Basin concept which is an all-inclusive concept; second, a less inclusive Indian Ocean Rim-Association for Regional Cooperation (IOR-ARC) scale. As with all regionalisms, there exist a variety of (often competing) economic and geopolitical motives both for constructing and for portraying the region in different ways or for creating different regionalisms at different scales.

Contested Regionalism

However, while regionalism can potentially fulfil a range of functions at different scales, there exist at least six sources of contestation. First, is the basic issue of whether regionalism is at all considered to be necessary or important. Second, contestation is likely to arise over the type of regionalism which is considered to be the most appropriate. Third, the geographical structure of regionalism is invariably contested – who should be members?, who should not?, and so on. Fourth, the goals of the regional grouping are likely to be internally contested. Fifth, states with overlapping regional membership may place themselves in cross-pressured situations which can adversely affect the internal coherence of regional groups due to goal conflicts. Finally, one source of ongoing concern within regional groupings is the extent of member equality. On the one hand, the dominance of one particular state in terms of regional decision-making can be a negative consideration for some member states. On the other hand, incorporating a dominant economic and political power within a regional grouping could facilitate market access and thus be of benefit to smaller states. Such a growth in regional economic interactions in turn might lead to greater regional institutionalisation. 'Egalitarian regionalism' is a concept which appears to be preferred in the Indian Ocean. This latter point touches on a potentially significant theoretical issue regarding the nature and functions of regionalism. One of the general arguments of Western neo-realists is that international economic cooperation is heavily dependent on the presence and efforts of a hegemonic leader. Among other things, the hegemon is seen as playing a key role in sustaining commercial and financial openness. Following this line of argument, we *should* observe regionalism to be developing more fully where a local hegemon is able to create and maintain regional economic institutions. We would also expect that regionalism would advance more slowly in those areas where local hegemonic leadership is less apparent. It has been suggested that, outside of the American context, that the presence of a regional hegemon is neither a necessary nor a sufficient condition for the emergence of successful regional economic or perhaps of any other types of regional institutions.

The Geopolitics of Australia's Regional Relations

Based on a composite set historical, colonial, security, cultural, trade, aid and other linkages, the geo-politics of Australia's regional relations has been characterised as operating on four broad fronts – in order of importance, a cooperative security front to the north, an aid front to the east, an environmental security front to the south and a trade front to the west.[4] Australia's perceived sphere of influence on the one hand –

a region *to which it can deliver* stability in the form of development assistance, and thus dominate, can be differentiated from Australia's regional orientation – a region *from which Australia takes* in the form of trade and investment and is thus dependent to a lesser or greater degree.

One of the most explicit considerations of Australia's regional geo-political priorities has been the identification of a "region of primary strategic interest" (ROPSI). This comprises two broad zones stretching from Coco Island in the west in an arc eastward around to New Zealand and to the South Pacific Islands and from the archipelago and island chain in the north to the Southern Ocean.[5] Australia's ROPSI in this characterisation incorporates Southeast Asia, the South Pacific and the eastern edge of the Indian Ocean, or, approximately 10 per cent of the earth's surface. It is instructive to consider how this region came to be a ROPSI. If we examine the history of Australian geo-political change, it is possible to identify three geo-political phases in Australia's existence as a state – a 'classical' phase in which Australia was a distant extension of Europe remote from global centres of power. While Australia looked West to Europe, it tended to "look past" India. Second, a Cold War phase when Australia was perceived to be threatened by the Soviet Union and located in an unstable Southeast Asia. During this period, Australia tended to look east across the Pacific towards the United States. Third, a post-Cold War phase in which Australia begins to emerge more as an independent geopolitical entity projecting more of its own interests rather than being subject to the interests of Anglo-European power.[6] This phase also saw Australia primarily looking north towards the Asia-Pacific region which, in former Australian Prime Minister, Paul Keating's view, *excluded* India.

The collective impact on Australia of cultural heritage, economic linkage and security ties has placed Australia to some degree in a conflictual triangular situation – culturally, Australia has close ties to Europe, economically, Australia is tied to the Asia-Pacific, and especially Northeast Asia, and the security relationship with the United States adds a third additional pull away from the Indian Ocean Region. One of the several difficulties faced by Australia's regional relations is what might be termed "territorial overstretch" – that is the ROPSI is so large that priorities had to be assigned to the sub-region which contained those states with historical linkages and over which Australia could be dominant – the "geopolitics of the backyard". The Indian Ocean Region thus assumed the role of Australia's "fourth front", after the north, east and south, and grudging acceptance of a 'western front' was driven primarily by Cold War concerns. Ironically, the end of the Cold War almost coincided with the 1987 decision to make the Australian navy a two-ocean navy. Thus, the "two ocean policy" came into existence.

Australia and the Launching of IOR-ARC

One recent commentator appears to be somewhat surprised that it took several years after the Cold War for countries in the Indian Ocean Rim to develop a regional grouping.[7] However, new regionalism came later to the Indian Ocean due to a combination of unique regional circumstances impacted upon by the global environment in a way that differed fundamentally from the context in the Asia Pacific Economic Cooperation arrangements.

The strength of intra-regional linkages around the Indian Ocean is now in its fifth principal stage. In the pre-colonial phase, for example, it has been argued that the Indian Ocean Region comprised a distinctive self-conscious "world" until it became incorporated into the global economy in the 18th and 19th centuries.[8] In the second colonial stage, while on the one hand, many of the economies around the Indian Ocean were restructured to meet extra-regional demands, generally as suppliers of raw materials for the industrialised North, on the other hand, intra-colonial contacts were maintained or generated during this period.[9] In the Cold War phase, the region was inevitably divided along ideological lines. Again, extra-regional forces militated against stronger intra-regional linkages. Nonetheless, the last decade of the Cold War period saw the development of several Indian Ocean sub-regionalisms. The fourth post-Cold War economic revival phase was also characterised by a slow process of adjustment and re-orientation away from ideological regionalism and towards economic regionalism. However, the current fifth phase of new regionalism was given an additional set of triggers comprising a combination of an increase in the intensity of globalised competition for scarce resources and an associated increase in the importance of globalised 'non-territorial' threats. As a result, never before has the necessity for inter-state regional and global cooperation been so great in the Indian Ocean.

Gareth Evans Indian Ocean vision

Australia's key strategic leadership role in the development of 'stage four' regionalism in the Asia-Pacific and in the Indian Ocean is reflected to some degree in its middle-power, intermediary role developed during the period when Gareth Evans was Australia's Foreign Minister, 1988-1996. Among other things, this role reflected the reality that Australia threatened no other state nor was threatened by any other state in the post-Cold War period. Evans possessed a particular vision of Indian Ocean regionalism that was based initially, but not exclusively, upon economic cooperation (Table 1).

Table 1. Gareth Evans Indian Ocean Vision

Economic complementarities
Tariff reductions
Forum for policy problems
Forum for peace and stability
Increased contact fosters regional identification
Inclusivity
Function by consensus
Multi-tracked
Broad agenda
Range of security issues
Research linkages
APEC as a model

Source: Evans 1995a; 1995b.

It was no coincidence that the Asia Pacific Economic Cooperation (APEC) grouping emerged at the end of the Cold War period in 1989. Since the Cold War divided the Indian Ocean Region, the shift from ideological to economic regionalism at the end of that period provided Australia a new and unique opportunity to help create and to build-upon developing regional economic linkages.

Australia was keen to engage *regionally* on all four fronts. Japan the dominant state behind the scenes in APEC with Australia as a front person. India was a dominant player, behind the scenes, with Australia taking a lead. Gareth Evans stressed the importance of Australia's relationship with India in his vision.[10]

The key 'Indian Ocean Triangle' states of Australia, India and South Africa (AISA) were the principal geo-political building blocks of an

Indian Ocean regionalism to ensure sufficient economic leverage as well as broad 'regional coverage'. However, India was slow in moving to a more open market-based economy and South Africa did not elect a majority democratic government until 1994.[11]

The regional implications of the collective changes to all three states meant that June 1995 was an appropriate and opportune time to host the International Forum on the Indian Ocean Region (IFIOR) in Perth. Unfortunately, from an acronymic perspective, *IFIOR* could not have implied a more tentative beginning.

Indian Ocean Regional Membership

Popular opinion would indicate that the collective of Indian Ocean states is *diverse* (and it is), and that the group was developed on a clean slate. In fact, the core grouping of states of the original Mauritius-initiated Indian Ocean working group process, which commenced March 1995, possessed a key common ingredient – that is, except for Oman, they were all members of the British Commonwealth – a residual 'British Lake' or a 'cricket alliance', perhaps? (Table 2).

Table 2. The Emergence of IOR-ARC Membership

The Core 7	The 1997 Additional Members	Joined in 1999
(Mauritius 1995)	(IOR-ARC formed Mauritius 1997)	
Australia#	Indonesia+	Bangladesh#
India#	Madagascar	Iran
Kenya#	Malaysia#+	Seychelles (withdrew 2003)
Mauritius#	Mozambique	Thailand+
Oman*	Sri Lanka#	United Arab Emirates*
Singapore#+	Tanzania#	
South Africa#	Yemen	

British Commonwealth member. *GCC member state. + ASEAN member state.

Australia was/is one of the Commonwealth's strongest proponents in the Indian Ocean Region for a range of reasons, not the least of which includes Australia's current preference not to be a republic and for the Union Jack to remain a part of its national flag.

Australia's influence was also evident in the model that was preferred for the creation of IOR-ARC – that is the APEC model. Australian experience as a founder member of APEC proved invaluable in providing as blueprint for a regional organisation in a region with relatively weak internal linkages, enormous diversity and a high level of economic insecurity.

IOR-ARC Becalmed

It seems that, after an initial burst of enthusiasm, Australian government interest in IOR-ARC waned relatively quickly. There appear to be a number of geopolitical and structural reasons why this occurred. Nonetheless, it is worthwhile to begin to evaluate the relative success or otherwise of IOR-ARC from various Australian perspectives.

The McPherson Evaluation

It is a salutary lesson to revisit an important critical evaluation of the performance of IOR-ARC that was presented by an Australian 'insider', Ken McPherson, at the inaugural IORG Conference in November 2002 (Table 3). McPherson was especially concerned that, after only three years, the academic and business groups had virtually ceased to function and had become "moribund". He was also concerned that the organisation, which he believed had been taken over by trade and foreign ministry officials, had become "dehumanised".[12]

Table 3. McPherson's Evaluation of IOR-ARC

1.	Vague IOR-ARC Charter
2.	Conflicting visions
3.	Weak commitment of member states
4.	System of governance unclear
5.	'Open' versus 'closed' regionalism?
6.	Membership conflicts
7.	Certain agenda items 'off limits'
8.	Impact of external events
9.	Bilateralism versus multilateralism
10.	Pre-eminence of domestic issues
11.	Reduction in resource commitment
12.	Lack of background in regional cooperation

Source: McPherson 2004.

After a rather critical evaluation of IOR-ARC, McPherson did offer some positive prescriptive suggestions, however. In particular, he called for the broadening of the IOR-ARC basis for cooperation; he suggested that IOR-ARC needed to tackle a wide range of issues which were seen to be of importance to Indian Ocean people, and he wanted regional governments to provide a stronger commitment to the business and academic groups.

Trade Linkages

In global terms, Northeast Asia (China, Japan and South Korea) is the 'centre of gravity' of Australian merchandise trade, accounting for almost half of the total in 2009-10. Australia's number one trading partner, China, alone accounted for 20.5 per cent of total merchandise trade. In contrast, for 2009-10, all 17 IOR-ARC states collectively accounted for one-fifth of Australian merchandise trade (Table 4). Indeed, six states were among Australia's top 22 trading partners – India (5th), Malaysia (11th), Singapore (7th), South Africa (22nd), Thailand (6th) and the United Arab Emirates (18th). In short, Australia's current trade links are relatively strong and growing with India, South Africa, UAE and all four ASEAN member states of IOR-ARC (Indonesia, Malaysia, Singapore and Thailand). However, trade with the other ten IOR-ARC states can be categorised as either relatively weak (Bangladesh, Iran, Mozambique, Oman and Sri Lanka) or relatively very weak (Kenya, Madagascar, Mauritius, Tanzania and Yemen). Indeed, imports into Australia from the relatively very weak trading states were negligible in 2009-10 (A$40.5M in total). It is very difficult to accurately evaluate the precise impact that IOR-ARC has had on Australian trade with the other 17 IOR-ARC states. However, if we assess the relative importance of total merchandise trade with Australia's *overall* trade performance we find that total trade with IOR-ARC increased from 9.07 per cent of the total in 1987-8 to 13.7 per cent of the total at the creation of IOR-ARC in 1997. In the 10 years following IOR-ARC, total merchandise trade increased to 18.61 per cent, and, as noted above, this has continued to increase (Table 5). It is clearly arguable as to whether Australian merchandise trade with IOR-ARC states would have increased irrespective of the creation of the regional grouping. In addition, the rate of increase in the relative importance of IOR-ARC states slowed somewhat after the creation of the regional grouping. Nonetheless, what is clear is that, in terms of Australia's merchandise trade, the relative importance of IOR-ARC to Australia has doubled in the period 1987-2007. However, Australian merchandise trade links with a number of IOR-ARC state members have remained relatively weak both before and since the inception of IOR-ARC (Table 5).

Table 4. Australian Merchandise Trade with IOR-ARC States 2009-10

Country	Exports (A$M)	Two main Australian exports	Imports (A$M)	Share of total trade	Global rank of total trade
Bangladesh	409	vegetables, wheat	122	0.1%	46th
India	16,179	gold, coal	1,846	4.5%	5th
Indonesia	4,326	wheat, live animals	4,687	2.2%	13th
Iran	149	medicaments, wheat	114	0.1%	59th
Kenya	30	wheat, manufactures	19	0.0%	91st
Madagascar	11.7	metals, pumps	5.5	0.0%	138th
Malaysia	3,127	petroleum, copper	8,483	2.9%	11th
Mauritius	103	meat, wheat	10	0.0%	73rd
Mozambique	321	machinery, clothing	1	0.1%	53rd
Oman	405	cars, live animals	66	0.1%	47th
Singapore	5,035	petroleum, gold	10,924	3.9%	7th
South Africa	1,762	coal, medicaments	1,004	0.7%	22nd
Sri Lanka	198	vegetables, dairy	106	0.1%	56th
Tanzania	90	wheat, metals	5	0.0%	75th
Thailand	4,707	gold, petroleum	12,441	4.2%	6th
UAE	1,974	cars, meat	2,294	1.1%	18th
Yemen	193	wheat, dairy	0	0.0%	65th
Total Australian merchandise trade with IOR-ARC states				20.0%	

Source: Australian Department of Foreign Affairs and Trade Website.

Table 5. Australian Merchandise Trade with IOR-ARC States 1987-2007

(% total merchandise trade)

	1987-8	1997-8	2007-8
Bangladesh	0.1	0.2	0.1
India	0.9	1.4	2.8
Indonesia	1.5	3.1	2.2
Iran	0.5	0.2	0.1
Kenya	0.01	0.02	0.02
Madagascar	0.001	0.001	0.003
Malaysia	1.5	2.5	3
Mauritius	0.05	0.05	0.03
Mozambique	0.004	0.01	0.1
Oman	0.1	0.1	0.1
Singapore	2.6	3.6	4.9
South Africa	0.3	0.9	1
Sri Lanka	0.1	0.1	0.1
Tanzania	0.004	0.02	0.01
Thailand	0.8	1.6	3.5
UAE	0.5	0.8	1.5
Yemen	0.1	0.1	0.05
Total	9.07%	13.70%	18.61%

Source: Australian Department of Foreign Affairs and Trade 2007.

Second Track Groups

Evaluating the degree of Australian success or otherwise in the second track groups – academic, business and tourism – is restricted somewhat by lack of data. Intuitively, the business group has been relatively successful and the tourism group has remained relatively weak and directionless. Data from the IOR-ARC Secretariat give some insight into the quantitative success of the Indian Ocean Rim Academic Group (IORAG). If we examine the Secretariat data for all 76 research projects initiated by the IORAG 1997-2010, we find that two states have been pre-eminently active in taking up the research leader/coordinator role – India (36%) and Iran (36%). Australia is fourth after Mauritius with 8 per cent of lead coordinating, with a two-thirds success rate, but all of these Australian-led projects were initiated in July 2000 or before. In short, in IORAG, Australia's leadership role has been essentially dormant for more than a decade, even though the status of the last project – University Student Mobility Programme for the Indian Ocean Region (UMIOR) – is indicated to be "ongoing".[13] However, current official Australian interest in UMIOR now appears to be non-existent.

Security Cooperation

While traditional security concerns were originally a part of Gareth Evans' IOR-ARC vision (Table 1), it appears that these matters were regarded as being too sensitive and thus essentially were seen to be off limits. In the Indian Ocean, therefore, security linkages and opportunities have tended to be bilateral rather than regional. For example, Australia and India have a strong mutual interest in maritime security cooperation.[14]

However, as has been recently argued, it is no longer possible for Indian Ocean states to continue to collectively ignore maritime regimes.[15] There is some evidence to indicate some success with regard to non-traditional security matters, especially in terms of maritime security and environmental security concerns. In the case of the latter, discussions on an Indian Ocean regional fisheries cooperation initiative using the Indian Ocean Rim Association for Regional Cooperation (IOR-ARC) as a basis appear to have been going on for several years. Some accounts claim that a Fisheries Support Unit (FSU) of IOR-ARC was created (or at least the concept was agreed) in 2005 and that its Headquarters was agreed to be in Oman in 2009. The FSU appeared on the Agenda of the last IOR-ARC meeting in Sana'a, Yemen in August 2010:

> 4.4.1.1 The Committee may recall that at the last Council of Ministers Meeting held in Sana'a on 25 June 2009, the Council adopted the text of the Memorandum of Understanding (MoU) for the Establishment of the said Unit of IOR-ARC and agreed that the Headquarters Agreement would provide further details regarding the budget provisions for the Unit. Malaysia submitted its views on the budget and finance of the Unit which was circulated to Sultanate of Oman.

Development Assistance

Since economic insecurity is a key commonality among Indian Ocean states, it has meant that the region has often been described as the 'heart of the third world'. Five IOR-ARC member states – Bangladesh, Kenya, Madagascar, Mozambique and Tanzania – have been recently classified by the World Bank as being among the poorest states on earth.[16] Some of these states have consequently become 'aid dependent'. For example, overseas aid was a significant percentage of total imports in 2005 for several IOR-ARC states with relatively weak or relatively very weak trade linkages with Australia – especially Kenya, Madagascar, Mozambique, Sri Lanka and Tanzania.[17]

It has been argued that Australian overseas development assistance (ODA) has been primarily designed to meet geo-political rather than human developmental objectives.[18] In other words, the global map of developmental need (with significant concentrations around the Indian Ocean Region) has not been matched by the geographical allocations per head of population of Australian aid. Rather, despite Australia's post-Second World War commitment to the Colombo Plan, Australian aid allocations have been subsequently directed primarily towards what has come to be known as Australia's 'arc of instability'.[19] Thus, rather than Australia looking *west* to the states of greatest economic need, in terms of aid receipts per head of population, Australia looked to regional states located within its perceived sphere of influence in order to maintain influence and to facilitate regional stability.[20] Consequently, Australian developmental linkages have tended to be weaker among Indian Ocean states and relatively strong in the Pacific Island States and Papua New Guinea. This is the so-called Southwest Pacific "aid front" associated with an "Australasian Monroe Doctrine" which emerged during the colonial period in the latter part of the 19th century, and which regarded the South Pacific Islands as an Anglo-Saxon preserve, into which other powers should not trespass.[21]

Thus, for 2008-9, the Pacific Islands States received 14.4 per cent of Australia's total aid budget, compared to 11.4 per cent to Indonesia, 10.1 per cent to Papua New Guinea, 9 per cent to South Asia and 4.5 per cent to Sub-Saharan Africa. IOR-ARC states collectively received 22.7 per cent of Australia's total aid allocation in 2008-9, with the five poorest IOR-ARC states together receiving just 2.2 per cent of Australia's development assistance.[22]

Back to the Ocean?

To Secure its Future, Australia must Look West as well as East (Rudd 2010)

Recent government statements have indicated a renewed Australian interest in the Indian Ocean Region and thus in IOR-ARC.[23] For example, in a speech in Perth in December 2010, Australian Foreign Minister, Kevin Rudd, outlined a renewed Australian vision for the Indian Ocean Region (Table 6). Apart from Australia's enduring strategic relationship with the United States, of particular importance in Australia's new look west and a new regionalism among Indian Ocean states have been both the rapid growth in India-Australia trade and a renewed interest in investment in and the 'mineralisation' of Africa.

Table 6. Kevin Rudd's Indian Ocean Vision

1. The Indian Ocean Region is undergoing profound transformation, both in economic and security terms.
2. Australia must look west, to the great challenges and opportunities that now present themselves across the Indian Ocean Region.
3. Energy security increasingly becomes a concern of national security.
4. Africa's economic significance is growing.
5. Australia's maritime zone is 8.5 million square kilometres and more than a third of this lies within the Indian Ocean Region. Australia has significant current and prospective energy and resource projects within this zone.
6. Australia's relationship with India is centrally important.
7. Australia will seek to improve institutional links with the Gulf Cooperation Council (GCC) and its member states.
8. Australia will work closely with India, as IOR-ARC Chair, to progress issues of relevance to IOR-ARC members, including fisheries management, customs training, energy security, and disaster management.

Source: Rudd 2010.

Overall, it has been suggested that the overall geopolitical significance of the Indian Ocean Region has shifted. As the post-Cold War globalised, non-ideological world has been in the process of reconfiguring, it has become increasingly preoccupied with new security challenges that in turn have had implications for the functioning and interests of the state. As noted earlier, these challenges include the necessity for inter-state cooperation to enable environmental security, an increase in competition for energy security, the security of sea lanes of communication, the rise of India and China, and a range of other traditional and non-traditional security threats.

Some commentators have suggested that the Indian Ocean is now in the midst of a "new maritime great game" between India and China and that it is not in Australia's interests for the region to become an arena for major power competition.[24]

Apart from a range of important domestic regional concerns, Australia's relationship with the United States is one of several additional key factors in the recent increase in Australia's interest in Indian Ocean matters. The United States has been undergoing a reassessment of the strategic importance of the Indian Ocean Region in recent years due in part to the growth in a range of non-traditional threats and since the growing economic and military importance of both China and India in the region clearly challenges US dominance in the region.[25] Indeed, it has been recently asserted that:

> … the Indian Ocean may be the essential place to contemplate the future of US power (Kaplan 2010, p. xiv),

and that,

> … Only by seeking at every opportunity to identify its struggles with those of the larger Indian Ocean world can American power finally be preserved (Kaplan 2010, p. 323).

It is well-known that the United States has generally eschewed regionalism and multilateralism in favour of bilateralism, unless states are territorially contiguous or within its own hemisphere. However, in the case of the Indian Ocean, the United States now appears to be in favour of a regionalism that might facilitate stability and may allow it to have some influence especially through its relationships with regional states, including Australia. Australia is thus 'strategically encouraged' to reignite its interest in Indian Ocean regionalism.

Conclusion

The combination of the change in the strategic significance of the IO, the emerging new security challenges and the re-realisation of the geographical fact that Australia *is indeed* an Indian Ocean state are eliciting a new Australian Indian Ocean policy response. Sam Bateman and Anthony Bergin, in an important and timely evaluation of Australia's Indian Ocean policies, have argued that Australia requires the implementation of a new vision for looking west which more closely recognises the new regional geo-political realities, which stresses increased regional engagement and which identifies key achievable priorities (Table 7).

Table 7. Bateman and Bergin's Indian Ocean Policy Priorities for Australia

- Fisheries management and marine research
- Improve dialogue with Indonesia on Indian Ocean matters
- Promote greater cooperation in the Eastern Indian Ocean
- Disaster relief, humanitarian assistance and people smuggling
- Increase development assistance to Africa
- Engage regional and extra-regional stakeholders
- Improve Indian Ocean policy coordination at all levels

Source: Bateman and Bergin 2010.

Such priorities require a strengthened engagement in IOR-ARC and a new approach underwritten by appropriate resources that guarantees a sustained long-term commitment. Part of this new approach will necessitate a comprehensive evaluation of the operations of all aspects of IOR-ARC, including its agenda, membership and organisational structure. In addition, Australia will need to call for a greater commitment to IOR-ARC on the part of all other member states, including the role of the Dialogue Partners. Certainly, the announcement by China of considerable additional financial support for the organisation in Yemen in 2010 indicates the beginnings of a renewed commitment of the Dialogue Partners. In Australia's case, however, there remains the ever-present geo-political constraint of the problem of "territorial overstretch" – of simply trying to undertake too much engagement across too great a span of territory on too many issues. The outcome of this will to a considerable degree depend on the nature of any reform agenda and the organisational (re)configuration of IOR-ARC, including its membership. In the final analysis, however, it will require Australia to identify key policy and regional priorities designed to maximise policy effectiveness.

End Notes

1. Commonwealth of Australia 2009, p. 37.
2. Beazley 2009.
3. Rumley 2005.
4. Rumley 1999.
5. Dibb 1986.
6. Rumley 1999.
7. Gupta 2010, p. 3.
8. McPherson 1993, p. 5.
9. Evans 1995a; 1995b.
10. Evans 1995a.
11. Rumley 1999, p. 231.
12. McPherson 2004.
13. IOR-ARC Secretariat 2010.
14. Commonwealth of Australia 2009, p. 96.
15. Gupta 2010, p. 272.
16. World Bank 2010, p. 305.
17. Editorial Essay 2010, pp. 11-12.
18. Rumley 1999, pp. 179-192.
19. Rumley, Forbes and Griffin 2006.
20. Rumley 1999.
21. Rumley, Forbes and Griffin 2006, p. 17.
22. AusAID 2009.
23. Rudd 2010.
24. Bateman and Bergin 2010.
25. Kaplan 2010.

References

AusAID (2009), *Australian International Aid Program, Statistical Summary 2008-2009*, Canberra.

Bateman, S. and Bergin, A. (2010), *Our western front; Australia and the Indian Ocean*, Strategy Paper, Canberra: Australian Strategic Policy Institute.

Beazley, K. (2009), 'Geopolitical power in the Indian Ocean', radio interview by Geraldine Doogue with Kim Beazley and Robert Kaplan that can be accessed at: http://www.abc.net.au/rn/saturdayextra/stories.

Commonwealth of Australia (2009), *Defending Australia in the Asia Pacific Century: Force 2030*, Defence White Paper, Canberra: Department of Defence.

Dibb, P. (1986), *Review of Australia's Defence Capabilities*, Canberra: AGPS.

DFAT (2002), *Direction of Trade Time Series 2000-01*, Canberra: Market Information and Analysis Branch.

Editorial Essay (2010), "Research agendas for the Indian Ocean Region", *Journal of the Indian Ocean Region,* vol. 6 (1), pp. 1-25.

Evan, G. (1995a), "The Indian Ocean Region: an Australian perspective", address to the Indian international Centre, New Delhi, 19 May, available at: http://www.gevans.org/speeches

Evans, G. (1995b), "Indian Ocean regional cooperation: exploring the possibilities", keynote address to the International Forum on the Indian Ocean Region, Perth, 11 June, accessible at: http://www.gevans.org/speeches.

Gupta, M. (2010), *Indian Ocean Region: Maritime Regimes for Regional Cooperation*, New York: Springer.

IOR-ARC Secretariat (2010), *All IORAG Projects (1997-2010) – Analysis*, Note 101122, Annex B, Mauritius.

Kaplan, R. D. (2010), *Monsoon: The Indian Ocean and the Future of American Power*, New York: Random House.

McPherson, K. (1993), *The Indian Ocean: A History of People and the Sea*, Delhi: Oxford.

McPherson, K. (2004), "The Once was an Ugly Duckling…", or; the sad history of the good ship IOR-ARC', in Rumley, D. and Chaturvedi, S., eds., *Geopolitical Orientations, Regionalism and Security in the Indian Ocean*, New Delhi: South Asian Publishers, pp. 112-119.

Rudd, K. (2010), 'Australia's foreign policy looking west', AusAID speech given at the University of Western Australia, 12 November 2010.

Rumley, D. (1999), *The Geopolitics of Australia's Regional Relations*, Dordrecht: Springer.

Rumley, D. (2005), "The geopolitics of Asia-Pacific regionalism in the 21st century", *The Otemon Journal of Australian Studies*, vol. 31 (1), pp. 3-25.

Rumley, D., Forbes, V.L. and Griffin, C., eds. (2006), *Australia's Arc of Instability: The Political and Cultural Dynamics of Regional Security*, Dordrecht: Springer.

World Bank (2011), *World Development Report 2011: Conflict, Security and Development*, Washington DC.

Chapter 7

Malaysia, Indian Ocean and IOR-ARC: Balancing Security and Economic Objectives

Ravichandran Moorthy

Introduction

The Indian Ocean is the third largest ocean in the world – with the size of twenty eight million square miles covering almost twenty per cent of earth's water expanse and lapping the shores of three continents in the most strategic waterways encompassing thirty littoral and eleven landlocked states, and with 1,284 islands. This region contains one third of the world's population, one quarter of landmass, and three quarter of strategic reserves of oil, iron ore and tin. In addition to its sheer size, the region has also experienced almost 70 per cent of world disasters, both natural and man-made. The states in this region are widely disparate in size, population, per-capita incomes and also in the composition of their societies. Some states are well developed while others are only 50 per cent literate.[1]

As an enormous water basin, the Indian Ocean borders land masses of Antarctica, Australia, Asia and Africa. It is also connected to other oceans and water masses by means of strategic waterways. In the west, it is connected to the Cape of Good Hope and the Red Sea, and in the East, to the Straits of Melaka – connecting it with the Malay and Philippines archipelagos, and the South China Sea. Its cosmopolitan characteristics as a result of centuries of seaborne trades and cross border interactions between various communities that borders its shores, made possible by its "narrow entrances and exits, vast and varied hinterlands, as well as climatic conditions favourable to both coastal and high-seas navigation",[2] have made the Indian Ocean interestingly unique and perhaps historically distinctive from other oceans. Since ancient times, geopolitically, trade linkages and diplomatic ties in the Indian Ocean were held together informally by inter-regional unities. McPherson argues that the convergence between communities in the West and in the East enabled the Asians, Africans and the Europeans to mingle, fight and trade over centuries, participating in complex structures of commerce and politics, supported by the systems of monsoon.[3] However, as Emrys Chew puts it, "it is only a matter of time before the balanced geography of the Indian Ocean gave rise to balances of power".[4]

Beginning from the end of the Cold War, the influences of security and non-security affairs in the Indian Ocean have steadily increased. The collapse of the Soviet Union brought an end to the confrontation of the Pakistan-China-United States (US) axis against the India-USSR axis. This era witnessed major realignment of security dynamics in the region to redress the perceived power imbalances caused by the increase of dominant and hegemonic powers. This development, coupled with India's meteoric rise as an economic powerhouse starting from 1990, saw many major powers such as the US, China, Japan, Russia and the European Union intensifying their engagement with the region. This raises many security and strategic questions – especially on how the changing dynamics of power relations will influence the geo-political equations and calculations in the region. According to Robert Kaplan, the Indian Ocean area will be the true nexus of world power and conflict in the coming years – it is here that the fight for democracy, energy independence, and religious freedom will be lost or won.[5] In his earlier writing in *Foreign Affairs* (March-April 2009), Kaplan notes that the Indian Ocean, which is already the world's energy and interstate seaways, will become strategically more significant in future. He claims that this region will be the stage for global struggles in the 21st century – with India and China have begun emphasising their sea power – thus, the job of managing their peaceful rise will eventually fall on the US Navy to a significant extent.[6]

The geo-political importance of this region has amplified especially in the context of the post-Cold War dynamics and the recent rise of

China. However, in spite of this higher visibility, the region has not been really successful in gaining universal acceptance as a geo-political entity. There are several reasons for this phenomenon – the first would plausibly be the effect of non-alignment movement in the immediate Second World War era. With the rise of the Cold War, many newly independent states, led by India, heeded the call for universal disarmament and the creation of the zone of peace in the Indian Ocean Region (IOR). This eventually spurred many countries in the region, namely India to adopt conciliatory and perhaps pacifist approach towards the Indian Ocean affairs. Arun Prakash claims that "feeble efforts have been made from time to time to create an IOR identity but they seem to be floundered either because of centripetal sub-regional forces or for fear of Indian dominance" – for example the Indian Ocean Rim Association for Regional Cooperation (IOR-ARC), a regional grouping formed in September 1997 for trade and economic cooperation has been a 'non-starter' for more than a decade.

Other initiative to engage the region, such as the Indian Ocean Naval Symposium (IONS) by the Indian Navy is still in its formative stage – more time is needed to gauge its impacts.[7] The second probable reason thwarting the IOR from acquiring its identity is the geographical classifications that were drawn up by the colonial masters. The lure of imperialism prompted many colonial powers to draw and redraw the land and sea boundaries of the world – in that process creating many new nations in parts of Africa, Asia and beyond. Geographical nomenclatures like the 'Near East', 'Middle East', 'South East Asia', and 'Far East', and lately the 'Asia Pacific' were given to identify non-Western regions. Some scholars have argued that such geographical classification has enabled the US to gain entry into Asia, not only as resident power, but also in terms of economic and military linkages between these regions.[8] Although the huge land and sea mass of the IOR is difficult to overlook, at least from a geographical angle, the region in itself has yet to develop into a political entity – to date it still remains a geographical entity. Perhaps for this reason, the recent move by India to promote the region as a 'geo-strategic' entity has drawn some concerns and suspicion from other IOR countries.

Some scholars have argued that countries like India, which is usually benign in terms of its engagements in the Indian Ocean, may be prompted, due to geo-political reasons, to assert more presence, if not dominance in the region. The worry is that India may be encouraged to embrace the 'neo-Curzonian' aspiration – Lord Curzon, the British Viceroy envisioned an empire centered in India. However, Arun Prakash argues that such an aspiration may have been overstated, because India's interests have been on creating external peace and tranquility in the region, so that it could concentrate on its massive socio-economic problems. As such, India's objective in the engaging the IOR is for keeping the region free of external intervention and conflict.[9]

The geo-politics in post-Cold War era has contributed to greater volatility in the security environment of the IOR. Over several decades, the region has witnessed numerous conflicts and tensions among states and with non-state actors both on land and on water. The region is home for two 'mutually unfriendly' nuclear weapon states – Pakistan and India. The Indo-Pakistan relations have been marred with repeated incidents of terrorists' violence and nuclear proliferation issues – amplifying security concerns in the sub-continent. In fact, the Indian Navy chief, Sureesh Mehta, has warned against terrorists potentially using shipping containers to transport nuclear weapons through the Indian Ocean waters, which apparently is the most frequented route used by proliferators – he postulates the need for comprehensive security measures against proliferation by sea.[10] In addition to proliferation issues in the sub-continent, the Iranian nuclear ambition and its persistent refusal to observe international non-proliferation norms, and the possibility of the resurgence of Iranian naval capabilities have increased security concerns in the IOR. The region has also been widely dubbed as the incubator of Islamic militancy and terrorism. The conflicts and unrest in Iraq, Afghanistan, Pakistan and other states suggest that the region will remain unstable in the foreseeable future.

With some 40 per cent of world oil and gas reserves, the region has been the stage for energy competition between major powers like China and the US. The region has been also characterised by growing strategic competitions involving both external powers and the littoral states – especially Beijing's increasing role in the IOR, the US interests to contain China, and India's agitation over Chinese presence in the so-called India's strategic backyard. Over the last decade, the Chinese have been paying closer attention to the IOR. China's special relationship with Pakistan and Burma, the proliferation of Chinese weapons of mass destruction (WMD) in South Asian states, and the growing presence of Chinese Navy in the Indian Ocean indicate China's growing interests to stake a claim in the IOR – some even have suggested that in the 21st century the IOR will be the template for Sino-Indian rivalry. The Chinese, however, refuted this assertion, saying that China adopts a benign strategy with regard to the Indian Ocean – focusing primarily on trade and development, good neighbourliness and friendship, and security and cooperation.[11] Since the Cold War, especially with regard to the Indian Ocean, China has moved on from the fear of encirclement by other states. However, a country like India, due to its territorial disputes with China, has remained fixated with the possibility of encirclement by the Chinese Navy in the Indian Ocean. This perception prompted many Indian security strategists to favour closer ties with the US – as a security balancer. For India, the geographical proximity of the Indian Ocean makes it natural and desirable of it to play a dominant role in the region. India's primary concern has been the protection of its 2.3 million square kilometers of Economic Exclusive Zone (EEZ), to secure energy supplies, promote overseas markets and to fulfill to its international commitments.

Over the last decade, other littoral states in the Indian Ocean have begun to put in place more pronounced policies of engagement with other states in the region. Malaysia, for instance, have begun to pay more attention to the Indian Ocean affairs – its active membership in the IOR-ARC is a testament of this interests. Strategically, the Indian Ocean has become increasingly important to Malaysia, especially as feeder waterway for sea line of communication (SLOC) to the Straits of Malacca and South China Sea. The constant increase of ships plying this route and the security risks posed by incidents such as trafficking, smuggling and piracy, has made the waterway among the most dangerous in the world. As a response to these threats, the Malaysians have set up a naval base in the island of Langkawi, in the approaches to the Indian Ocean.

Observed externally, the IOR presents a big 'chaotic' picture – with a host of military, economic and religious disarray occurring in the countries that share its coastline. Notwithstanding this, such observation fails to discern the commonalties that have bounded the regions together.

For centuries, the Indian Ocean has been an important centre for the interactions of great civilisations – its waters have transported world's major religions, cultures and traditions, languages, value systems and people across numerous shores of this ocean – allowing for the fusion of cultures between them.[12] In Southeast Asia, the people from the Indian Ocean have been interacting with the communities in the Malay Archipelago and mainland Southeast Asia for many centuries. Archeological and historical evidences show that trading activities and early settlements have begun as early as the third century BC. The Indian merchants were already familiar to sea-borne trade and travel in rough seas as early as the third to sixth century BC. The numerous voyages made by Indian merchants to Southeast Asian ports were recorded in *Rig Veda Samhita*, a collection of Vedic Sanskrit hymns.[13] In fact, the *Jatakas*,[14] confirmed that by the second century AD, Indian influence had already rooted in parts of the Peninsula, Indo-China and the Archipelago.[15] The intensity of interactions between these regions increased during the Christian era with constant movement of traders and priests between the Indian sub-continent and numerous city-states of Southeast Asia. The traffic eventually led to the establishment of a cross-cultural link between the Indian Ocean and Southeast Asia. This laid the foundation for the growth of several city-states in the region and paved the way for the 'Indianisation' of the Malay way of life.[16] Before the coming of Islam in early 15th century, the Hindu-Buddhist traditions dominated the Malay world through structures of government, thoughts and philosophy, religious pursuits and civilisational influences. Much of the local practices and languages have been greatly influenced by these traditions – evident till today in many communities in Southeast Asia. Subsequently, after Islam became more dominant in the Malay courts and later being elevated as the official religion for the newly independent nations like Malaysia, Indonesia and Brunei, the Indian influence gradually reduced – overtaken by Islamic teachings.

Malaysia and the Indian Ocean

Prior to the participation in the IOR-ARC, Malaysia did have a concerted policy regarding its engagement with the Indian Ocean region. Malaysia has been managing its relations with the countries in this region bilaterally and through other multilateral forums. The lackadaisical attitude towards this region is perhaps that Malaysia never really saw itself as being part of the Indian Ocean fraternity. Although much part of the history of Malaysia and the Malay Archipelago has been constructed by the 'Indianisation' of belief systems, language, cultural practices, and societal norms and values, Malaysia has remained fairly disengaged from the Indian Ocean, especially with the Indian sub-continent for several decades after independence in 1957. Another probable reason for this attitude is India's initial lack of interests in engaging Southeast Asian countries due to its historical affinity with the West, and the pre-occupation with the 'neighbourly' problems that besieged the sub-continent for decades. While there are many regions within the Indian Ocean Rim, for Malaysia, the Indian sub-continent affairs usually take precedence over the other parts. As such, it is interesting to note that Malaysia's attitude towards the region can be analysed based on its relations with the sub-continent, especially with regard to both India and Pakistan. In this paper, I have argued that Malaysia's relations with India and Pakistan have been based on the principle of 'equi-distance'– in order to balance Malaysia concerns over several geopolitical issues in the region, and at the same time not to be seen as overly favouring any particular side on those issues.

Malaysia-India Relations

Both Malaysia and India share similar experiences in their struggle for independence from the British. As a result of colonial legacies and baggage, both countries started off from being heavily western-centric in their approaches to administration and international relations, but later they sobered down into accepting the reality of the changing geo-political dynamics of their respective regions. Having a substantial minority of ethnic Indians taking up citizenship in Malaysia, and sharing similar experiences on pluralism and nation building issues, both countries managed to maintain cordial relations over several decades. Nevertheless, in the Cold War era, it appeared that Malaysia and India belonged to different and opposing blocs of ideology. Malaysia and several other ASEAN countries were seen to be more pro-Western and support the anti-communist stance – this is resulting from Malaysia's experience with communist insurgency between 1948-1960 and the general worry of many ASEAN countries of the spread of communism to other parts of the region after the fall of Vietnam. For India, the regional security dynamics and the emerging threats to its sovereignty by unfriendly neighbours prompted it to favour relations with the communist Soviet Union. It was for this reason that Malaysia and several other ASEAN countries adopted a 'cautious strategy' with regard to their relations with New Delhi in the early years of the Cold War. However, Soviet's non-committal attitude with regard to the Kashmir issue and the Chinese invasion of Ladakh, was a rude awakening on the part of India of the futility of 'over reliance' on Soviet support. This scenario encouraged a change in attitude – evident in India's post-Cold war relations.

Despite being veiled by the Cold War curtain, Malaysia-India relations never really went through bumpy road. India was among the first few countries that Malaysia had established diplomatic relations with, and in the late 1960s, Indira Gandhi's government openly supported Malaysia on the issue of Sabah – a territory in Borneo that joined the newly independent Malaya, also claimed by the Philippines as being part of its territory – a claim that is still in place till today. Malaysia-India bilateral relations further improved with the support for the 'non-alignment' initiatives. The inculcation of the Non-Alignment Movement (NAM) in 1955 brought out the spirit of reducing of the influence of super power rivalries and the liberation of countries of the Third World from the clutches of colonialism. Both Malaysia and India supported this policy as an important pillar of their foreign policy engagement, especially in managing their interactions both from within and outside their regions. Further, India's endorsement of the ASEAN's Kuala Lumpur Declaration of the Zone of Peace, Freedom and Neutrality (ZOFPAN) in 1971, was also seen as an enhancement of the non-alignment 'spirit' in the Southeast Asian region as well as endorsement of the convergence of foreign policy interests between India and ASEAN. As such, Malaysia-India relations in the Cold War period can be easily categorised as upholding the NAM principles, as both countries realised that mutual peace and security can only be achieved from the observance of these principles. For India, with Malaysia, Indonesia and several other ASEAN member countries supporting the NAM principles, this regional outfit became an important regional ally for India's initiatives.

In the post-Cold War period, when super power rivalries were no longer the main issue of concern, NAM was still kept relevant by its members by transforming itself to pursue other agendas in the new strategic environment, especially in the broader global context. New issues such as addressing global inequalities became points of convergence between the interests of both Malaysia and India – clearly manifested in the discourse of South-South cooperation, more prevalent in the economic interactions. In terms of security, the post-Cold War exhibited a rather tumultuous period for Southeast Asia, as countries grapple to manage their inter-state relations into new and sometimes 'untested' alliances and groupings – thus creating new 'security dilemmas' in the region.

There was a 'reasonable' worry that the post-Cold War dynamics may have given rise to other regional powers, such as India, China or even Japan, who may be tempted to fill the power vacuum in the region – a situation greatly disfavoured by the ASEAN countries. While Malaysia sees China's engagement with the region with some level of apprehension, especially with regard to China's more aggressive behaviour in managing their territorial claims over Spratly Islands, the Indian side seems to project itself as a responsible benign power where ASEAN is concerned. While in an overall perspective both countries enjoy cordial and fruitful relations, there are still several persistent issues that influence Kuala Lumpur's stance towards New Delhi, especially in balancing Malaysia relations between India and Pakistan.

In the past Malaysia has raised concerns over the need for India to address the Kashmir issue with Pakistan in a responsible way. Being an Islamic country and prominent member of the Organisation of Islamic Conference (OIC), Malaysia adopted the OIC's positions with regards to Kashmir and issues faced by the Muslim minority in India, especially with regard to the Babri mosque debacle. In the same light, several incidents of ethnic clashes in Malaysia namely the Kampung Medan incident in 2001 and the HINDRAF rally in 2007 generated public outcry among the people of Tamil Nadu in south India, with several Tamil politicians openly criticising Malaysia's ill-treatment of its ethnic Indian minority. On the issue of nuclear, given the strong anti-nuclear stance of Malaysia and ASEAN, Malaysia condemned India's nuclear test in 1998.

Notwithstanding these issues and incidents, Malaysia continues to view India as a friendly power, and relations between these countries have remained cordial over the years. India is vital to balance the rise of China, especially in response to China's increasing interests in the Straits of Malaka, South China Sea and the Indian Ocean. This can be seen in Malaysia's support of India's participation in ASEAN led-processes such the ASEAN Regional Forum, where India is a member. India's democratic system, its large middle-class society, rising naval presence in the Indian Ocean and coupled with its rising economy makes it an important global and regional player that could not be ignored.

Malaysia-Pakistan Relations

Malaysia's relation with Pakistan has been quite bumpy especially in the early years of Malaysia's independence. Initially, Pakistan was not in favour of the establishment of the Federation of Malaysia in 1963,[17] throwing its diplomatic support to Indonesia who opposed the formation of Malaysia and the merger of the states *Sarawak* and *Sabah* (both former British colonies in the island of Borneo) with the federation. Despite the Cold War dynamics, the two countries have interacted in numerous settings and forums, especially in the Commonwealth, the OIC and D-8 platforms. Pakistan's unstable democracy and military coups have distanced Malaysia from giving its full support to Pakistan. This scenario further exacerbated when Pakistan joined forces with the US in the global war on terror, which prompted Kuala Lumpur to exercise caution in engaging Islamabad. However, relations gradually improved with the changing geo-politics of the region. Being a Muslim country, Malaysia continues to engage and support Pakistan in numerous initiatives including supporting its entry into several regional organisations, both at the inter-governmental and track-two levels.[18] Malaysia also exercised caution in dealing with the issue of Kashmir, as it did not want to agitate the Indian side. Although not as aggressive as India, Pakistan's economic development had opened up many avenues for trade, investment and business opportunities for Malaysia.

In 2007, Malaysia and Pakistan signed the Malaysia-Pakistan Closer Economic Partnership (MPCEPA), a trade pact to further strengthen their economic, trade and industrial cooperation for the long-term. This was Malaysia's first bilateral free trade agreement (FTA) with an OIC country. In addition to tariff cuts, the FTA agreement with Pakistan covers liberalisation in trade, in goods and services, investment, as well as bilateral technical cooperation and capacity building in areas such as sanitary and phyto-sanitary measures, intellectual property protection, construction, tourism, healthcare and telecommunications. Malaysia's total trade with Pakistan in 2006 amounted to RM 3.306 billion comprising exports worth RM 3.089 billion and imports RM 217 million. In 2007, total trade amounted to RM 3.243 billion comprising exports of RM 3.016 billion and imports RM 227.3 million.[19]

Notwithstanding the economic importance, with the Commonwealth's mandate, Malaysia had 'politely' advised the Pakistani military leadership to return to democracy. On the nuclear issue, Malaysia's position is the same with regard to India – it condemns Pakistan's nuclear tests that have heightened security concerns in the sub-continent. Malaysia has also repeatedly urged both India and Pakistan to take the road of non-proliferation. After the 9/11 incident, Pakistan emerged as US's important ally in the global fight against terrorism – much to the displeasure of many countries, including Malaysia. However, Malaysia has not been openly critical on this issue for the reason that it was also pressured into supporting the US initiatives, especially in the area of maritime terrorism, cases of extradition and intelligence cooperation.[20] In the post-Cold War era, relations between these two countries generally improved – evident in numerous high level visits both at the heads of state, senior officials and top military brass. For example, the visit by Najib Razak (the then Malaysian Defence Minister) to Pakistan in 2001, managed to wrap-up an arms deal worth more than USD 100 million for the purchase of anti-tank and surface-to-air anti-aircraft missiles from Pakistan. In the area of training and development, Malaysia has been forthcoming in assisting Pakistani officials in human capital development through various technical assistance programme. In time of need, such as the 2005 earthquake that shook Pakistan, the Malaysian government provided some RM 21.6 million worth of aid to Pakistan – this figure does not include private sector contributions.[21]

On the whole, it can be concluded that despite the initial set back in relations in the late 1950s and early 1960s, Malaysia and Pakistan have enjoyed relatively good relations over the last several decades. Commonalities in terms of the solidarity of the Muslim *ummah* have further strengthened the resolve of both countries to foster closer ties. This 'spirit' was aptly mentioned by Abdullah Ahmad Badawi, the 5th

Prime Minister of Malaysia in his address to the Malaysia-Pakistan Business Forum in Islamabad, Pakistan in 2005.

> I would like all of you to know that at the inter-governmental and diplomatic levels, Malaysia and Pakistan have very good relations. We have no bilateral political or diplomatic problems between us. Our two countries share similar perceptions and positions on most current and important international issues. This stems from the fact that we have many shared historical traditions, that our people share the same religion and that both Malaysia and Pakistan share common membership of international organisations which are important to developing countries. These include the Organisation of Islamic Conference. Indeed, Malaysia and Pakistan have cooperated on many international issues. I must, however, point out that our bilateral economic and trading relations are not at par with our political and diplomatic relations. This imbalance must be corrected. The potentials do exist for expanding and deepening the relations in these two areas. In fact, there is still so much that our two countries can offer not only to each other but also to the world at large.[22]

Malaysia's current foreign policy initiatives with regard to both Pakistan and India have been largely driven by economic imperatives. As a trading nation, Malaysia constantly looks for economic collaborations and business opportunities for Malaysian enterprises. Pakistan's recent economic rise, although not as rigorous as India, has opened new avenues for business opportunities and partnership in many areas of development. Malaysia also sees Pakistan as a responsible player in international relations especially through its involvement in platforms such as the OIC and D-8.

Malaysia and IOR-ARC

The IOR-ARC is a regional arrangement for economic cooperation among countries that borders the Indian Ocean. It was formed in March 1997 with 14 member states, which includes Australia, India, Indonesia, Kenya, Madagascar, Malaysia, Mauritius, Mozambique, Oman, Singapore, South Africa, Sri Lanka, Tanzania, and Yemen. IOR-ARC was formed based on the concepts of open regionalism – modelled after the Asia Pacific Economic Cooperation (APEC). The proponents of the Indian Ocean regionalism, namely India, Australia and South Africa were motivated by the fervour that regional cooperation in the Indian Ocean would be economically beneficial. IOR-ARC came into being in the backdrop of the rise in regionalism worldwide, especially North American Free Trade Arrangement (NAFTA) and APEC, and countries like India and Australia felt the need to exert their regional leadership through this grouping.

What is 'open regionalism'? In essence, open regionalism involves regional economic integration without discriminating economies outside the region. Integration is facilitated by the "removal of barriers to and the encouragement of regional cooperation without discrimination against outsiders".[23] Quite the opposite, the 'discriminatory regionalism' entails "preferential trading arrangements, free trade areas, and customs unions, where official trade barriers for members are lower than for non-members".[24] Open regionalism was first expressed in the Pacific Economic Cooperation Council (PECC) in 1980 as a precursor for future economic development in the Asia-Pacific region. The concept was later adopted in 1989 at its first inaugural meeting. It took APEC nearly 30 years to come into being after the initial discussion of economic regional cooperation, and almost a decade for the adoption of the open regionalism model. In contrast, the IOR-ARC, the second grouping to adopt this model, came into being almost instantaneously, without any serious efforts to engage in economic cooperation in the past.

Some scholars have argued that the haphazard manner of the formation of IOR-ARC is perhaps the primary reason for this grouping to be slacking in their regional cooperation initiatives. Despite the setting up of the Indian Ocean Commission in Mauritius to oversee the development of this grouping, no significant development has materialised – some have even claimed that this grouping is moving closer towards natural disintegration. There is also a well-established realisation that despite sharing the same ocean, the region is just too diverse in terms of geography, cultures and systems, for open regionalism model to the meaningfully implemented.

The IOR-ARC is non-political; it focuses on the enhancement of cooperation in specifically three areas – trade and investment, business and education. In addition to these stated areas of focus, new areas such as 'disaster risk cooperation' have gained importance, especially in the wake of several natural calamities such as the Asian tsunami that obliterated the coastline of several Asian countries and the recent Fukushima nuclear disaster. Malaysia's involvement in IOR-ARC can be termed as 'low key', but it has been actively participating in all initiatives and engagements, especially in seminars and education promotions. In the area of education, Open University Malaysia (Malaysia's premier distance learning university) has offered three scholarships for masters level courses on design and technology to IOR-ARC member countries. Another Malaysian university – Universiti Kebangsaan Malaysia (UKM), a lead partner in the IOR-ARC academic group, has reiterated its commitment to host a convention for the establishment of 'IOR-ARC Centre for Multilateral Education' at UKM.

However, the implementation of these initiatives has been abysmal – the agencies concerned have blamed the foreign ministry for not providing clear policy direction and the resource allocation for implementing the initiatives. Another reason for this situation is the lack of interests among Malaysian academics to conduct research about the Indian Ocean region. Malaysia also supports other educational initiatives like the University Mobility Programme (UMIOR).

There are also initiatives led by other IOR-ARC countries that receive Malaysia's support – such as responding to the threat of piracy in the Indian Ocean – an initiative led by Yemen and Oman with the cooperation from International Maritime Agency. For Malaysia, the IOR-ARC has similar importance with the BRIC countries (Brazil, Russia, India and China), especially in terms of economic development and opportunities in trade, investment and business. The importance of this region to Malaysia was clearly reflected with the appointment of Samy Vellu (the former Minister of Works) as the special envoy with ministerial status to India. Malaysia also sees its membership in IORARC as an extension of its South-South Cooperation initiative started 1990's during Dr Mahathir Mohammed's administration – the policy promotes the enhancement of mutual cooperation and benefit among states of the South.

Although the IOR-ARC was formed on the basis of regional economic cooperation objectives, the geo-political dynamics of the region, especially in the post-Cold War period, makes it unfeasible to keep politics out of this regional outfit. It should be noted that the IOR-ARC has been 'led' by countries like India and Australia and to a lesser extent South Africa. These countries, as a result of their geo-political and economic interests, see the Indian Ocean as a region that they could exert their regional leadership. Australia's economic interests and India's increasing naval presence, and coupled with the presence of major powers like the US and China in the Indian Ocean, have prompted other countries in the region to view this regional outfit with some level of caution. Pakistan, another important player in the region has stayed out of the grouping. Malaysia's 'low key' engagement in this grouping has been based on the desire not to get embroiled in the politics of the region.

One area of the serious concern to Malaysia is the increase of incidents of piracy in the Indian Ocean and Strait of Malacca, which have directly impacted on the security of sea lanes in these regions. Through the IOR-ARC, Malaysia would like to see greater collaborative initiatives among Indian Ocean countries to combat this menace effectively. The security of the sea lanes is not only important to the littoral states, but also to major powers like Japan and China whose economies are largely dependent on sea trades and energy supplies transported by sea. For this reason, both Japan and China have been supportive of regional initiatives to manage the threats of piracy in the Strait of Malacca and South China Sea.

Conclusion

For Malaysia, the affairs of the Indian Ocean have become increasingly important to its foreign policy and economic objectives. As the region becomes more cohesive and interdependent, Malaysia's 'low key' engagement in the region will eventually evolve into active participation. Malaysia sees that the region holds enormous opportunities in terms of trade, investment, business and education – also not forgetting cooperation among developing economies through the South-South Cooperation initiative. In order to facilitate cooperation in the region, the IOR-ARC needs to play a more creative and active role through a variety of programmes of engagement as stipulated in its areas of focus. At present, despite the well established recognition of the geo-political and economic importance of this region to the world, the IOR-ARC's performance as a regional grouping has been abysmal. One reason for this weakness is the lack of political will and commitment on the part of its member states, where IOR-ARC's projects have been given low priority by policy makers. With limited governmental support for its initiatives, IOR-ARC's projects remain "ambiguous, sporadic and fragmented, leading to a 'stop and go' pattern of regional cooperation".[25]

At present, IOR-ARC lacks firm commitment to push for a meaningful advancement towards regional economic cooperation. Given this reality, it is futile for IOR-ARC to insist on the 'open regionalism' mode of operations, based on the APEC model – as these groupings do not share similar background and foundations. As stated in its founding Charter, IOR-ARC should seek to promote the 'spirit of multilateralism' through mutually beneficial cooperation among its members based on a consensus-based, evolutionary and non-intrusive approach.[26] Therefore, in order to reinvigorate the grouping, the IOR-ARC should first become a forum to develop the spirit of regional economic cooperation. It should embark on serious efforts in seeking commitment and sustained dialogues with member states, and encourage a regional environment favourable for the promotion of trade and investment. Such initiatives would lay the groundwork for more ambitious economic activities and cooperation between member states in future.

END NOTES

1. Mihir Roy, "Maritime Security in South West India", *http://www.iips.org/Roy-paper.pdf,* accessed 4 March 2011.
2. Emry Chew, *Crouching Tiger, Hidden Dragon: The Indian Ocean and the Maritime Balance of Power in Historical Perspective,* Working Paper No.144, S. Rajaratnam School of International Studies, Singapore, 25 October 2007, pp.1-2.
3. Kenneth McPherson, *The Indian Ocean: A History of People and The Sea,* Oxford University Press, New Delhi, 1999, pp. 1-15.
4. Ermry Chew, *Crouching Tiger, Hidden Dragon: The Indian Ocean and the Maritime Balance of Power in Historical Perspective*, p.iii.
5. Robert D. Kaplan, *Monsoon: The Indian Ocean and the Future of American Power*, Random House, New York, 2010, p. 9.
6. Robert D. Kaplan, "Center Stage for the 21st Century: Power Plays in the Indian Ocean", *Foreign Affairs,* March/April 2009; *Also see* Arun Prakash, "Introduction", in C. Uday Bhaskar and Kamlesh K. Agnihotri, eds., *Security Challenges along the Indian Ocean Littoral: Indian and US Perspectives,* Matrix Publishers, New Delhi, 2011, p. 1.
7. Arun Prakash, "Introduction", in C. Uday Bhaskar and Kamlesh K. Agnihotri, eds., *Security Challenges along the Indian Ocean Littoral: Indian and US Perspectives,* Matrix Publishers, New Delhi, 2011, p. 2.
8. Ibid. p. 2.
9. Ibid. p. 3.
10. A. Vinod Kumar, "India Should Take Leadership Role in Indian Ocean Region",

http://www.boloji.com/index.cfm?md=Content&sd=Articles&ArticleID=4919, accessed on 5 July 2011.

11. Rockin Th. Singh, *Security in the Indian Ocean Region: Role of India*, Vij Books India Pvt. Ltd., New Delhi, 2011, p. 3.
12. Arun Prakash, "Introduction", p. 5.
13. Kernial Singh Sandhu, *Early Malaya*, University Education Press, Singapore, 1973, p. 1. *See also*, P. Wheatley, *The Golden Khersonese*, University of Malaya Press, Kuala Lumpur, 1961, pp. 177-179.
14. Refers to the collection of fables – many concerning former lives of Buddha.
15. Sandhu, *op.cit.*.
16. Kernial Singh Sandhu, "Indian Settlement in Melaka", in Kernial Singh Sandhu and Paul Wheatley, eds., *Melaka: The Transformation of A Malay Capital c.1400-1980.* vol.2, Oxford University Press, Kuala Lumpur, 1983, p. 174. *See also,* Ravichandran Moorthy, "The Evolution of the Chitty Community", *JEBAT*, vol. 36, 2009, p. 6.
17. In 1963, the Federation of Malaysia came into being, with territories like Sabah (the former British North Borneo), Sarawak and Singapore joining the then Malaya. Later in August 1965, Singapore pulled out from the Federation and became an independent state.
18. K.S. Balakrishnan, "Malaysia-Pakistan Relations: Understanding International Relations in the Muslim World," *The Journal of Diplomacy and Foreign Relations*, vol. 11, no. 1, 2010, p. 28.
19. Bernama. com, "Malaysia, Pakistan Sign FTA," November 12, 2007, http://www.bernama.com/bernama/v3/news_lite.php?id=295643, accessed on 2 May 2011.
20. K.S. Balakrishnan, *op. cit.*, p. 30.
21. Anon, "Najib strikes multi-million ringgit weapon deals from Pakistan," *New Straits Times*, 1 February 2001.
22. Abdullah Bin Haji Ahmad Badawi's speech at the Malaysia-Pakistan Business Forum, Islamabad, Pakistan, February 16, 2005, Speech Collection Archives of the Chief Executives, http://www.pmo.gov.my/ucapan/?m=p&p=paklah&id=2923, accessed 3 May 2011.
23. Ross Garnaut, "A New Open Regionalism in the Asia Pacific", http://www.rossgarnaut.com.au/Documents/A%20New%20Open%20Regionalism%20in%20the%20Asia%20Pacific%202004.pdf, accessed 6 July 2011.
24. Rockin Th. Singh, *Security in the Indian Ocean Region,* p. 36.
25. Ibid. p. 53.
26. The Indian Ocean Rim Network, "The Charter of the Indian Ocean Rim - Association for Regional Cooperation", http://www.iornet.com/iorarc/charter.htm, accessed 3 May 2011.

Chapter 8

Rescaling Indian Ocean Regionalism in the Era of Climate Change: Perspectives *on* and *from* the Bay of Bengal

Sanjay Chaturvedi

Introduction

India takes over from Yemen as the Chair of the Indian Ocean Rim Association for Regional Cooperation (IOR-ARC) at a critical juncture in its evolution since 1997.[1] The regional grouping which focused on the Indian Ocean *Rim* finds itself at the crossroads today. It is faced with challenges arising out of multiscalar transitions and transformations in an era of climate change and scarcities (e.g. commodities, water and clean environment) on the one hand, and a growing mismatch between conceptual-theoretical formulations and practices of 'regionalism' in international relations on the other. Exigencies arising out of 'transnational' flows and networks and the interdependency/dependence interface of hierarchical-asymmetrical international political economy in the neo-liberal era, further underline the need for broadening and deepening the nature and scope of IOR-ARC beyond 'economic' cooperation.

The new Charter of the IOR-ARC[2] (replacing the old 1997 Charter) reiterates the value of "historical bonds created through millennia among the peoples of the Indian Ocean Rim and with a sense of recovery of history" while acknowledging "economic transformations and speed of change the world over which is propelled significantly by increased intensity in regional economic cooperation".[3] The new Charter defines "IOR-ARC Region" as "the territories of the Member States", permits membership of the Association to "all sovereign States of the Indian Ocean Rim which subscribe to the principles and objectives of the Charter and are willing to undertake commitments under the Charter" and excludes "bilateral and other issues likely to generate controversy and be an impediment to regional co-operation".[4] And the objectives of the Association are "to promote the *sustained growth and balanced development of the region and of the member states*, and to create *common ground* for regional economic cooperation; to focus on those areas of economic cooperation which provide maximum opportunities to develop *shared interests* and reap mutual benefits. Towards this end, to formulate and implement projects for economic cooperation relating to trade facilitation and liberalisation, promotion of foreign investment, scientific and technological exchanges, tourism, movement of natural persons and service providers on a non-discriminatory basis; and the development of infrastructure and human resources, inter-alia, poverty alleviation, promotion of maritime transport and related matters, cooperation in the fields of fisheries, trade, research and management, aquaculture, education and training, energy, IT, health, protection of the environment, agriculture, disaster management" (emphasis given).[5]

The central argument in this chapter is that the unfolding dynamics and dilemmas of climate change underline the urgency of rescaling Indian Ocean 'regionalism and 'regional cooperation'. Climate change is likely to question not only the *rim*-centric definition of region followed by the IOR-ARC as "territories of the Member States" but also the concepts, definitions and assumptions of the key objectives of the Association. Besides analysing what IOR-ARC *can* and *should* do to mitigate climate change and its adverse effects including human displacements/migrations, food/water insecurities, we also need to examine what climate change might do to the IOR-ARC and some its foundational principles and objectives. With the old state-centric cartographies becoming increasingly outdated in the era of climate change and growing scarcities, both the classical geo-politics and orthodox economics need to be replaced by ecological politics and welfare economics in pursuit of comprehensive transboundary collaborative plans of action in various parts of the IOR.

The new approach to Indian Ocean regionalism in turn calls for a critical and much more nuanced understanding of both space and scale in the IOR. As Anssi Paasi[6] puts it so succinctly, "scales are not fixed, separate levels of the social world but, like regions/places, are structured and institutionalised in complex ways in de/reterritorialising practices and discourses that may be partly concrete, powerful and bounded, but also partly unbounded, vague or invisible. Scales are also historically contingent; they are produced, exist and may be destroyed or transformed in social and political practices and struggles. The institutionalisation/deinstitutionalisation of region, place and scale are in fact inseparable elements in the perpetual process of regional transformation".

It is not a question of *whethe*r but *when* the IOR-ARC, in a serious and systematic manner, will be taking on its agenda the multi-dimensional, multiscalar challenge of climate change. My intention in this chapter is not to engage in the scale debate *per se*, but to provoke a debate on a theoretical starting point from which to approach and explore the nature of policy challenges that complex spatial-geographies of climate change are likely to pose before the IOR-ARC and its member states and societies. Despite near consensus among political geographers that scale is neither given nor fixed, and is socially constructed, fluid and contingent, several questions demand further critical reflection in the context of climate change.

At what regulatory scale (sub-national, national, supra-national) should the various aspects of the problem of climate change be approached, understood and addressed in the Indian Ocean; the Ocean of the Global South? What are the implications of various representational modes (including metanarrative[7]) or discursive frames of scale for mitigating climate change and devising strategies for adaptation through cooperative frameworks?

The chapter begins with a brief overview (taking a few examples from Mozambique and Bangladesh) of how climate change is likely to undermine the human-environmental security and displace 'political economy of life'[8] in the IOR. The section to follow provides an overview of the impacts of climate change on the Indian Sunderbans, drawing largely from a recent WWF India report.[9] The concluding section of the chapter reflects on the larger implications of climate change for the foundational principles and objectives of the IOR-ARC and argues that in the times to follow, this one and only regional initiative may have to look for a new multiscalar paradigm of cooperation driven by both a new, people-centric economics and a new ecological politics.

In-between the Himalayas and the Antarctic: Mapping Climate Change in the Indian Ocean Region

Both by virtue of its location on the world ocean map and ecological-geographical layouts, the Indian Ocean and its various parts, inter-connected through delicately inter-locked ecosystems, are going to be affected both by the melting of the Himalayan glaciers in the north and the Antarctic ice cap down south. This, in my view, is a good example of how ecological reasoning and interconnections can, and do, collapse physical-geographical distances. The 2009 SCAR Climate Change and the Environment Report provides a comprehensive assessment of the implications of 'Antarctic climate change' on the 'rest of the world'.[10] On the Antarctic Peninsula nearly 87 per cent of glaciers are decreasing and the one that are increasing are doing so only due to increased regional precipitation. 'By 2100 West Antarctic ice sheet may discharge enough ice to raise sea level up to 1.4 m (+) with a significant challenge for Antarctica and for coastal populations across the globe'.[11] Jan-Gunnar Winther of the Norwegian Polar Institute has pointed out that, 'the impacts of climate change in the polar regions over the next 100 years will exceed the impact forecasts for many other regions and will produce feedback with significant global consequences'.[12] The semi-enclosed seas of the Indian Ocean, the low lying littorals of the Bay of Bengal like Bangladesh, and the islands like Maldives, are going to bear the major brunt of climate change. It is rather difficult to fathom the scale of such skewed geographies of global warming and all that it entails, as detailed by the IPCC.

It is in the executive summary of Chapter 6 entitled, 'coastal systems and low lying areas' that Working Group II of the Fourth Assessment Report of the IPCC[13] talks about the following (reproduced verbatim) six important policy-relevant messages: 'Coasts are experiencing the adverse consequences of the hazards related to climate and sea level (very high confidence)'; 'Coasts will be exposed to increasing risks, including coastal erosion, over coming decades due to climate change and sea level rise (very high confidence)'; 'The impact of climate change on coasts is exacerbated by increasing human-induced pressures (very high confidence)'; 'Adaptation for the coasts of developing countries will be more challenging than for coasts of developing countries due to constraints on adaptive capacity (high confidence)'; 'Adaptation costs for vulnerable coasts are much lesser than the costs of inaction (high confidence)'; 'The unavoidability of sea level rise, even in the longer-term, frequently conflicts with present-day human development and trends (high confidence)'. The above-mentioned policy-oriented statements, marked by different levels of 'confidence', are backed up by facts and figures. Here are just a few citations from the executive summary.[14]

The number of those 'exposed' to tropical cyclone hazards annually in different parts of the globe is about 120 million, out of which 250,000 people were killed between 1980 and 2000. We are told that, 'The anticipated climate-related changes include: an accelerated rise in sea level of up to 0.6 m or more by 2100; a further rise in sea surface temperatures by up to 3 degrees centigrade; and intensification of tropical and extra-tropical cyclones; larger extreme waves and storm surges; altered precipitation/run off; and ocean acidification. The phenomena will vary considerably at regional and local scales, but the impacts are virtually certain to be overwhelmingly negative'.[15] Furthermore:

> Increased flooding and the degradation of freshwater, fisheries and other resources could impact hundreds of millions of people, and socio-economic costs on coasts will escalate as a result of climate change ... Populated deltas (especially Asian megadeltas), low lying coastal urban areas and atolls are key societal hotspots of coastal vulnerability, occurring where the stresses on natural systems coincide with low human adaptive capacity and high exposure. Regionally, South, South-east and East Asia, Africa and small islands are most vulnerable ... Without adaptation, the high-end sea-level rise scenarios, combined with other climate changes (e.g. increased storm intensity), are as likely as not to render some islands and low lying areas unviable by 2100 ... Sea level rise has substantial inertia and will continue beyond 2100

> for many centuries. Irreversible breakdown of the West Antarctica and/or Greenland ice sheets, if triggered by rising temperatures, would make this long-term rise significantly larger, ultimately questioning the viability of many coastal settlements across the globe.[16]

Climate change in the IOR has a complex spatial-geography to its both in terms of causes and consequences. As Dennis Rumley puts it so aptly, "climate change issues place most Indian Ocean states in a complex conundrum since the overall causes of greenhouse gas emissions vary both by level of economic activity as well as economic development".[17] In terms of absolute global emissions, China, the United States and the EU remain at the top of the table. As many as eight IO states are among the world's top 20 greenhouse gas emitters, namely Australia, India, Indonesia, Iran, Malaysia, Saudi Arabia, South Africa and Thailand. According to Rumley,[18] "Since the top 20 emitters produce more than 80 per cent of global emissions, then the Indian Ocean states are responsible for approximately 40 per cent of all greenhouse gas output. Furthermore, since the growth in emissions is currently projected to be greatest among states of the developing world, then the Indian Ocean Region is likely to become a greater emissions source over the next century".[19]

As far as the consequences of climate change for the IOR are concerned, the complex and compelling overall regional context of underdevelopment demands and deserves critical attention. At the same time, it is neither feasible nor desirable to detach or divorce the issue of climate change from the longstanding history of ecological degradation and deeply entrenched ecological irrationalities in a vast majority of these polities. A number of scholars have cautioned therefore against the casual and uncritical deployment of the rhetoric of climate change coming from international organisations in general, and multilateral financial institutions in particular, to the Indian Ocean Region. Eero Palmujoki deserves serious attention when he points out that, "IOs (International Organisations) use economic rhetoric in their arguments in the issues dealing with climate change. The use of economic concepts suggests that global issues can be translated into economic language, a transcendent way to persuade actors in the governance of environment and development. The dominance of economic rhetoric reflects the failure of comprehensive efforts to mitigate and adapt the climate change through global convention based on sovereignty and environmental justice".[20] Also marginalised by the anthropogenic climate change discourses anchored in 'global' scale are the alternative (not necessarily confrontationist) political, social-cultural, and ethical discourses on ecologically sustainable development. Many such alternative perspectives remain skeptical of 'global governance' rhetoric and underline the importance of 'down scaling' the discourse of climate change to 'subordinate' levels, in order to focus the dynamics and dilemmas of communities and localities in Global South. What follows next is a short engagement with multiscalar nature of a few select examples from Mozambique and Bangladesh, which appears to reinforce the point made by Ian Bailey and others that it is difficult to assign "rigid spatial scales or hierarchies to certain processes (e.g. climate change), whether to determine political jurisdictions or simply to make phenomena comprehensible".[21]

Least developed countries of the IOR, such as Mozambique, are confronted with challenges that are likely to be missed out by climate change metanarrative, which, while privileging the 'global' over other scales, tend to conceal one of the key ethical issue related to climate change, namely the capacity (rather the lack of it) of least developed countries to mitigate and adapt. For example, there is a candid official acknowledgement of the fact that,

> There are only four dams build in Mozambique in the southern regions, which have been built to control floods and supply people with water, including irrigation. However, *there is a lack of qualified personnel to deal with the control and evaluation of river levels through the use of modern technology. Capacity building initiatives will enable better assessments of river related hazards, and will enable the reduction of negative impacts from changes in water levels.*[22] (emphasis given)

As further underlined in the National Adaptation Programme of Action of Mozambique, the capacity of the family farmers to deal with the adverse effects of climate change is quite low.[23] This fact assumes critical importance in the light of the fact that agriculture, livestock and fisheries are the most important sectors of Mozambique economy, with agriculture representing nearly 80 per cent of the country's labour force. As far as the coastal communities of Mozambique are concerned, they lack the capacity to mitigate and adapt to climate change. In a globalising world, where time and distance are perceived by many as

> 'collapsing', physical geography still matters a great deal in climate change mitigation and adaptation. For example, Mozambique, with an extensive coastline, marks the western limit of the cyclone and tropical storms active zone.[24] As a result, it is affected by tropical cyclones and other disturbances at regular intervals which place significant constraints on development initiatives targeted towards poverty reduction. Mozambique has also suffered due to regular droughts, which have seriously undermined efforts towards sustainable development. It is to state the obvious that the country is vulnerable to catastrophes and that the risks posed by climate change would aggravate absolute poverty in Mozambique and make it increasingly difficult to realize millennium development goals.

One of the key and compelling rationales behind realising the vision of 'maritime regionalism' for the IOR relates to the fact that the anticipated adverse consequences of climate change (e.g. floods, droughts and human displacements) will defy the 'national' boundaries of IOR-ARC member states (as well as the non-member states) both on land and at sea. In other words, the Indian Ocean of the Global South and its communities (especially the poor and the marginalised) will have to bear the brunt of adverse climate change consequences. It is the east coast of Africa in particular that demands and deserves the critical attention of IOR-ARC with a sense of urgency. The example of Mozambique is amply illustrative of how climate change is likely to act as a multiplier for long-standing human-ecological insecurities in the region.

In the African continent, Mozambique has the third longest maritime coast extending about 2,700 square kilometers.[25] The labyrinth of delicately interlocked ecosystems is characterised by estuaries, dunes, mangrove forests, coastal lakes, banks and coral reefs, marine weed and swamps. These critical habitats for various species of ecological importance and economic value are no doubt highly vulnerable to climate change. At the same time the social and economic activities that are being developed along the coast such as fisheries, port exploitation, tourism and sports as well as mining, oil and gas (which are still under development), represent a significant value and sustain the livelihoods of over 60 per cent of the people residing in the first 50 kilometers of the country's continental coastal zone.[26] On the other hand, the land based activities in coastal cities of Mozambique such as the manufacturing of raw-material along regional rivers (transboundary waterways shared by the upper and the lower riparian states), are resulting in diminishing water levels and increasing sediment content, which in turn contribute significantly to the reduction of water quality and quantity. The negative impact of such ecologically unsustainable 'development' activities on transportation, erosion, marine invertebrate's productivity, the fishery sector and ecological tourism demand serious and early interventions. These adverse impacts are further exacerbated by the lack or inefficient treatment of industrial and domestic wastes, which are often discharged directly into rivers and seas; a harsh reality to be observed in various other parts of the IOR.

Bangladesh, largely by virtue of its geographical/geo-political location, is widely perceived and reported as one of the most vulnerable countries to climate change-induced sea level rise.[27] It is difficult to deny that for coastal states such as Bangladesh, tropical cyclones, with major economic, social and environmental consequences, have always been a major challenge. Countries that are most exposed for example, China, India, the Philippines, Japan, Bangladesh have densely populated coastal areas, often comprising deltas and mega deltas.[28] Every year, up to 119 million people are on average exposed to tropical cyclone hazard.[29] From 1980 to 2000, out of a total of more than 250,000 deaths caused by tropical cyclones worldwide, nearly 60 per cent occurred in Bangladesh alone. Even this figure is less than the 300,000 killed in Bangladesh in 1970 by a single cyclone. Although according to the IPCC,[30] Bangladesh remains one of the 'key hotspots of societal vulnerability in coastal zones' due to 'highly sensitive coastal systems where the scope for inland migration is limited'. 'Most of the land area of Bangladesh consists of the deltaic plains of the Ganges, Brahmaputra and Meghna rivers. Accelerated global sea level rise and higher extreme water levels may have acute effects on the human population of Bangladesh (and parts of West Bengal, India) because of the complex relationships between observed trends in SST over the Bay of Bengal and monsoon rains, subsidence and human activity that has converted natural coastal defenses (mangroves) to aquaculture'.[31]

On 26 September 2009, Sheikh Hasina, the Prime Minister of Bangladesh, in a speech delivered at the 64th Session of the United Nations General Assembly, spelt out the implications of climate change for her country.[32] She not only made a reference to millions of 'climate migrants' and 'climate refugees' but also underlined the need for an international legal regime. Her narrative, ably supported by natural science evidence, is visibly marked by fear and anxieties:

> Climate change has for some time been adversely impacting our low lying, deltaic, monsoonal country. Though Bangladesh's contribution to climate change is negligible, it is one of its worst victims. Erratic floods, cyclones, droughts and earthquakes are interrupting our agriculture, and challenging our water resources, health, energy, urban planning, etc. Cyclones, battering the coastal areas, have particularly been taking countless lives, and sudden floods uprooting families in thousands, year around. River bank erosion, landslides, soil degradation and deforestation are causing millions of climate change refugees. They are already all over our thickly populated cities. What is alarming is that a meter rise in sea level would inundate 18 per cent of our land mass, directly impacting 11 per cent of our people. Scientific estimates indicate, of the billion people expected to be displaced worldwide by 2050 by climate change factors, one in every 45 people in the world, and one in every 7 people in Bangladesh, would be a victim. Rapid, unplanned urbanisation, occupational dislocations, food, water and land insecurity are some of the consequences of climate change. The affected communities would not only lose their homes, they would also stand to lose their identity, nationality, and their very existence, and in some cases, their countries.[33]

Prime Minister Sheikh Hasina, in her message to the 'Bangladesh Climate Change Strategy and Action Plan 2009', further expressed the resolve of her government to 'free' the people of her country from the 'terror of climate' and to ensure that 'people are fully protected from its adverse impacts as promised in our manifesto'.[34] However, the following excerpt from the report seems to suggest that the government of Bangladesh has already arrived at the conclusion that 'more than 20 million' displaced Bangladeshis will be migrating to other parts of the world:

> It has been estimated that there is the impending threat of displacement of more than 20 million people in the event of sea-level change and resulting increase in salinity coupled with impact of increase in cyclones and storm surges, in the near future. The settlement of these environmental refugees will pose a serious problem for the densely populated Bangladesh and migration must be considered as a valid option for the country. Preparations in the meantime will be made to

convert this population into trained and useful citizens for any country.[35]

The quotation above raises a number of questions[36] that the IOR-ARC will have to consider at some stage in order to pursue proactive and effective regional policy responses an extraordinarily complex issue-area. Who are environmental refugees? Who among the anticipated millions of displaced Bangladeshis, 'in the event of sea-level rise', for example, would qualify to be 'environmental refugees' and why? Is there no difference whatsoever between 'climate refugees' and 'environmental refugees'? What are the grounds for assuming that those displaced due to either sudden onset of natural disasters or gradually unfolding climate change or even abrupt climate change would necessarily choose to cross the national borders in search of safety and survival? Jean-Francois Durieux, Deputy Director, Division of Operational Services at the United Nations High Commissioner for Refugees (UNHCR), is reported to have said, 'The risk of mass migration needs to be managed. It's absolutely legitimate for Bangladesh and the Maldives to make a lot of noise about the very real risk of climate migration; they hope it will make us come to their rescue. But reopening the 1951 convention would certainly result in a tightening of its protections. ... The climate in Europe, North America and Australia is not conducive to a relaxed debate about increasing migration. There is a worry doors will shut if we start that discussion'.[37] As far as the countries of the Indian Ocean region are concerned, especially the Bay of Bengal littorals, the ethical-moral imperatives and political exigency arising out of them will make it increasingly difficult to simply 'shut' the doors on those displaced by climate change in immediate or even extended neighborhoods. After all, the ground reality is that there is a glaring mismatch between ecological spaces and territorially bound spaces of national sovereignties, and the 'boundary' between the two is likely to be breached by both human and non-human flows induced by the climate change.

Growing Mismatch between the Ecological and the Geopolitical Spaces: The 'Indian' and the 'Bangladeshi' Sunderbans

The Indian Sundarbans Delta (ISD) is part of the delta of the Ganga-Brahmaputra-Meghna (GBM) basin in Asia. The Sundarbans, shared between India and Bangladesh is home to one of the largest mangrove forests in the world. The ISD, the western a part of the complete GBM delta, is spread over about 9,630 square kilometres.[38] Larger (eastern) part of the Sunderbans delta lies in Bangladesh. It was the silt carried by the river Ganges as well as its tributaries like Mayurakshi, Damodar, Ajay, and Kansai rivers that formed the GBM delta between 2500 and 5000 years ago. Human settlements are to be found on 54 deltaic islands (spread over a little over half of the area) and the mangrove vegetation covers the remaining part. Especially during the pre-monsoon period (and from September through November) the ISD is exposed to extreme storm events. Extreme weather events, such as severe storms or cyclones, have been historically observed at frequent intervals. According to the WWF India,

> A pronounced ecological change is evolving in this delta due to huge discharges of untreated domestic and industrial effluents carried by tributary rivers as well as the disposal of contaminated mud from harbour dredging and resulting from the rapid emergence of the Haldia Port Complex, a major oil disembarkment terminal in eastern India. The Sundarbans delta has become susceptible to chemical pollutants such as heavy metals, organochlorine pesticides, polychlorinated biphenyls and polycyclic aromatic hydrocarbons which may have changed the estuary's geochemistry and affected the local coastal environment. As home to a significant portion of one of the world's largest contiguous block of mangrove forests, the portion under natural vegetation in ISD holds a prominent global place and a part of it has been designated as UNESCO World Heritage site in 1987 in recognition of its high biodiversity as well as the occurrence of endangered and highly threatened species, including the only population of tigers found in a coastal mangrove habitat.[39]

The most prominent feature of the ISD is the mangrove ecosystem that dominates the landscape and defies the geopolitical boundaries between India and Bangladesh. Nearly 85 per cent of all mangrove habitats found in India lie in the ISD. At least seven of these mangrove species or species group are threatened and require immediate conservation measures. Both the direct human activities and natural environmental changes are responsible for the degradation of natural ecosystems in the ISD. As far as the impacts of climate change on other components of the natural environment are concerned, except for changes in the physical components, "there is insufficient knowledge to attribute changes directly to climate change".[40] While emphasising that much more interdisciplinary research is the need of the hour, the WWF Report points out that,

> The pattern of governance in the ISD has so far struggled to keep up with the management and development challenges posed by this complex system. Given the disproportionately heavy impact that climate change is expected to have on this delta area, the need to improve adaptive management and develop more appropriate solutions for this unique system has become acutely urgent. Changes, in the face of climate change, are required in the broader context of physical limitations of a delta system, national development and human settlement management, biodiversity conservation, and transboundary cooperation. Putting the ISD in perspective and accounting for this broader context will be crucial if correct management decisions are to be made. If current policies and patterns of development continue, the ISD is likely to face steep and insurmountable challenges in coping with the pressures of predicted changes, particularly in the face of population growth and impacts of climate change. To date, the gravity of these challenges has not been publicly recognised. *The ISD is in need of early, proactive and informed interventions by all actors involved in the management and development of this area, especially the state and national governments.* The growing consensus among a vast body of scientists and experts from all over the world is that unless highly informed and sometimes bold changes in policy and governance are introduced, coping with the pressures of predicted changes will be nearly impossible. *In view of the grave situation facing the ISD and the fact that without much needed change, this environmentally and economically important area is rapidly heading towards an uncertain future...*[41] (emphasis given).

The widely cited findings of a study on the Sunderbans, carried out by Dr. Sugata Hazara, Director, School of Oceanographic Studies, Jadavpur University, revealed as early as 2006 that Lohachara Island (once inhabited by ten thousand people) had simply vanished and nearly two-thirds of Ghoramara Island had been permanently inundated due to sea level rise. Those displaced from the Lohachara Island fled to an island called Sagar, which is said to be equally vulnerable, already having lost 7,500 to rising sea levels.[42] Ghoramara Island has been attributed by some to both natural and human disasters, including climate change induced sea level rise. As the poor communities loose their homes, land and fields and exposed to multiple displacements, irrespective of which side of the Sunderbans they are (Indian or

Bangladeshi), they would demand and deserve transboundary cooperation at sub-regional and regional levels.

Concluding Reflections: Rethinking Space and Scale in Indian Ocean Regionalism

I have argued in this chapter that the IOR-ARC is at the crossroads, with a number of alternative futures beckoning the inhabitants and communities of the Indian Ocean region in the era of climate change and scarcities. What kind of future will prevail is likely to be decided to a large extent by the imagination and representation of the *'Indian Ocean space'* that this one and only architecture of multilateral cooperation chooeses to place at the heart of its visualisation of 'regional' cooperation. A territorialised, predominantly state-centric representation of Indian Ocean space might result in a rather thin regional cooperation that remains prisoner of 'national' scale and the concomitant definition of 'Indian Ocean Region' as constitutive of (and constituted by) the "territories of member states". On the other hand, visualising Indian Ocean as a fluid, multi-dimensional space, formed by the ongoing multiscalar linkages and interactions among states, civil societies and ecosystems, is likely to open new spaces for innovative forms of regionalism. In short, the issues of space and scale remain critically important both to the present and future of Indian Ocean regionalism and demands further reflection and research.

I have also argued that it is equally important to explore further the implications of climate change for the theory and practices of regionalism in the Indian Ocean, as currently being subscribed to by the IOR-ARC. At the heart of such exploration is the need to critically engage with the ongoing debate on the 'climate as political space', insightfully initiated in a seminal article by Eva Lovbrand and Johannes Stripple.[43] Their contention is that despite widespread de-territorial representations of greenhouse gases flowing in to the atmosphere and resulting in 'global warming', in both popular and scientific discourses, "international climate policy has resulted in a territorialisation of the carbon cycle".[44] While the de-territorial, trans-boundary nature of the atmosphere takes borders out of the equation, the territorialising nature of state-centric geo-political discourses on 'national sinks' puts them back again. In their view, "there seems to be a tension (quite palpable throughout the Indian Ocean region[45]) between the spatial constructions of climate space as global, transnational and territorial, and a political resolution that tends to reframe it in nationalist/statist terms".[46]

As briefly outlined in this chapter, perspectives *from* the Sunderbans in the Bay of Bengal seem to suggest that a new and nuanced social construction of the Indian Ocean space as an 'inter-regional arena' (to borrow the term from Sugata Bose[47]) is needed for realising ecologically sustainable, socially just and equitable development of the region; in short the 'political economy of life'. From an ethical-normative perspective, the 'global' environmental-climate change demands thinking and planning for 'security' in ecological terms in the Anthropocene.[48]

Philip Steinberg has shown in his seminal study[49] how the Indian Ocean space has also been subjected to various social constructions from time to time, including those of 'strategic void' and 'a maritime battlefield'.[50] Such constructions stand reinforced today as Indian Ocean is being subjected to post-Cold War rounds of militarisation.[51] According to Steinberg, "The Ocean is not simply an environment wherein distinct marine phenomena may be observed by marine specialists (i.e. marine geographers). Rather it is a space that, like land, shapes and is shaped by, a host of physical and social processes".[52] Steinberg therefore underlines the importance of taking into account "the geography of *ocean-space*, a term that is intended to capture both the specificity of the world ocean and the fluidity between the study of landward and seaward domains, as both are socially and physically constructed through linked dynamics".

The fast changing fluid geographies of Indian *Ocean-space* in the era of climate change demand and deserve new imaginations and social constructions. The characterisation of Indian Ocean-space as 'inter-regional space' by Sugata Bose is most relevant in my view, especially in the context of climate change. Bose recalls how during the course of his visit to India in 1995, Nelson Mandela, articulated a vision for cooperative architecture of multilateralism centered on the Indian Ocean Rim, by duly acknowledging the "natural urge of the facts of history and geography"; an expression found in the IOR-ARC Charter.[53] To quote Bose,

> In promoting the formation of an Indian Ocean Rim Association for Regional Cooperation (IOR-ARC) to bring together the littoral countries from South Africa through India to Southeast Asia, he had the right idiom and the wrong instruments. He had touched a historical cord that harped back to a cosmopolitan harmony, but regional organisation made up of nation-states did not possess the necessary skills to play that music. Yet the tune is embedded in the not too deep recesses of memory and history of the peoples of the Indian Ocean arena, and it is one, if it can be expressed and embellished, they will know how to enjoy.[54]

The "embedded cosmopolitan"[55] approach to Indian Ocean regionalism in general and climate change mitigation and adaptation in particular, questions the abstract, disembodied, globalised, and depoliticised concept of the cosmopolitan realm[56] and enables us to represent the voices and perspectives *from* the peoples and places (especially those on the periphery) in the Indian Ocean region.

Climate change, despite being increasingly framed by many in alarmist terms of a threat multiplier, also provides an *opportunity* to reclaim the multiscalar spatiality of "postcolonial conversations" and "interplay of multiple and competing universalisms" with the help of which the peoples of the Indian Ocean region could historically turn the Indian *Ocean Space* into an interregional arena.[57] Furthermore, says Bose, "It was this task of creating hybrid and polyphonic languages of translation that the peoples of the Indian Ocean interregional arena had so successfully accomplished through the archaic and modern phases of globalisation. It remains the only hope for a new (embedded) cosmopolitanism in a postcolonial setting".[58]

It has not been my intention in this chapter to privilege one scale over the other. On the contrary, I have sounded a note of caution against such a practice, which, I believe, could result in a clash of scales inhibiting innovative, proactive and holistic responses to climate change. A multiscalar, overlapping and fluid socio-cultural-political *spatiality* of climate change cannot be captured by the classical, fixed geographical scale, with neatly marked aggregated levels ranging from 'local' to 'global'. Mahatma Gandhi once talked about majestic oceanic circles, i.e. about the independence of the grassroots. According to Gandhi, centralised government is inherently prone to violence. By contrast, he advocated the decentralisation of political power. The same could apply to the governing arrangements at the regional and global scales. Explaining his metaphorical vision of the structure of a future non-violent society, Gandhi wrote: "Life will not be a pyramid with the apex sustained by the bottom. But it will be an oceanic circle whose centre will be the individual always ready to perish for the village, the latter ready to perish for the circle of villages, till at last the whole becomes one life composed of individuals, never aggressive in their arrogance, but ever humble, sharing the majesty of the oceanic circle of which they are integral units".[59] What is important here for the purposes of my argument is the contrast between the inclusive spatiality and the horizontal spacing of the 'oceanic circles' of Gandhi's geographical imagination of political economy of life (highly pertinent with regard to the IOR) and the exclusive spatiality and the vertical spacing of the various competing, often colliding, conceptualisations of state-centric space and scale. An unorthodox imagination of 'scales' as 'circles' might open up new intellectual spaces in pursuit of various building blocks for 'maritime regionalism' by a reinvigorated IOR-ARC.

A first vital step in this direction could be the setting up of a Task Force on Climate Change Mitigation and Adaptation by the Indian Ocean Rim Academic Group (IORAG), in collaboration with the Indian Ocean Research Group (IORG). The mandate of the proposed task force could be to map out, in a comparative perspective, climate change national action plans, and related institutional-policy landscapes, of the IOR-ARC member states and identify the areas where transboundary collaborative policies and action plans are the urgent and compelling need of the hour. The recommendations of the task force might act as a catalyst for debating and devising more ambitious, proactive, multiscalar and transboundary responses by the IOR-ARC to climate change.

End Notes

1. The current membership of the Association includes: Australia, Bangladesh, India, Indonesia, Islamic Republic of Iran, Kenya, Madagascar, Malaysia, Mauritius, Mozambique, Sultanate of Oman, Singapore, South Africa, Sri Lanka, Tanzania, Thailand, UAE and Yemen.
2. Third Draft (1 August 2010), Charter of the Indian Ocean Rim Association for Regional Cooperation (IOR-ARC) Sana'a, Republic of Yemen, IOR/2SCSO/REP/10/1.6.
3. Ibid.

4. Ibid.
5. Ibid. The remaining objectives, largely within the political economy framework, include: to explore all possibilities and avenues for trade liberalisation, to remove impediments to, and lower barriers towards, free and enhanced flow of goods, services, investment, and technology within the region; to encourage close interaction of trade and industry, academic institutions, scholars and the peoples of the Member States without any discrimination among Member States and without prejudice to obligations under other regional economic and trade co-operation arrangements; to strengthen cooperation and dialogue among Member States in the fields of fisheries, trade, research and management, acquaculture, education and training, energy, IT, health, protection of the environment, agriculture, disaster management.
6. Anssi Passi, "Place and Region: Looking Through the Prism of Scale", *Journal of Progress in Human Geography*, vol. 28, 2004, pp. 28: 542.
7. See Greg McCarthy, "The Climate Change Metanarrative, State of Exception and China's Modernisation", *Journal of the Indian Ocean Region*, vol. 6, no. 2, 2010, pp. 252-266. Jean-Francois had announced in his seminal work titled "The Postmodern condition: A Report on Knowledge" (1992) the death of 'metanarrative' as a totalising system of knowledge with claims of foundational truths with universal applicability. Greg McCarthy would disagree on the ground that what Jean-Francois had described as the key defining features of a metanarrative can be found in the dominant Western discourses of climate change. These three major characteristics are as follows. Among various competing discourses one that is likely to qualify as metanarrative needs a story/narrative that can go beyond its own scientific/epistemic community and make itself intelligible to both politicians/policy makers and the community at large. Secondly, it is crucial that the narrative itself becomes inextricably intertwined with the scientific knowledge that it draws on, so that scientific narrative not only gets legitimised through rule-making and rule-implementing institutions but also transforms itself through this process into a truth claim without an author subject. Finally, such intimate intertwining of science and politics tends to evoke a sense of powerful 'global' and globalising moral justification, persuading communities (irrespective of their location on the face of the globe) to act in a particular (ethical manner) in the 'best interests of humankind'.
8. Here by acknowledge the insights shared by Professor Jyrki Kakonen, Jean Monnet Professor at University of Tallinn, Estonia.
9. Danda, Anamitra Anurag, Gayathri Sriskanthan, Asish Ghosh, Jayanta Bandyopadhyay and Sugata Hazra, *Indian Sundarbans Delta: A Vision*, World Wide Fund for Nature-India, New Delhi, 2011.
10. Turner, J., Bindschadler, R., Convey, P., di Prisco, G., Fahrbach, E., Gutt, J., Hodgson, D., Mayewski, P., and Summerhayes, C.ed., *Antarctic Climate Change and the Environment*. Cambridge: SCAR, 2009, Executive Summary, p.xxvi–xxvii.
11. Ibid.
12. ATCM, Report from Antarctic Treaty Meeting of Experts on Implications of Climate Change for Antarctic Management and Governance: Co-Chairs' Executive

Summary with Advice for Actions. XXXIII Antarctic Treaty Consultative Meeting, 3-14 May, Punta del Este, Uruguay, 2010, p. 63.

13. Nicholls, R.J., Wong, P.P., Burkett, V.R., Codignotto, J.O., Hay, J.E., McLean, R.F., Ragoonaden, S. and Woodroffe, C.D, "Coastal systems and low-lying areas. Climate change, impacts, adaptation and vulnerability", in M.L. Parry, O.F. Canziani, J.P. Palutikof, P.J. van der Linden and C.E. Hanson, ed., *Contribution of Working Group II to the Fourth Assessment Report of the Intergovernmental Panel on Climate Change*, Cambridge University Press, Cambridge, 2007, pp. 315-356.
14. Nicholls, R.J., Wong, P.P., Burkett, V.R., Codignotto, J.O., Hay, J.E., McLean, R.F., Ragoonaden, S. and Woodroffe, C.D, "Coastal systems and low-lying areas. Climate change, impacts, adaptation and vulnerability", in M.L. Parry, O.F. Canziani, J.P. Palutikof, P.J. van der Linden and C.E. Hanson, ed., *Contribution of Working Group II to the Fourth Assessment Report of the Intergovernmental Panel on Climate Change*, Cambridge University Press, Cambridge, 2007, pp. 317-318.
15. Ibid.
16. Nicholls, R.J., Wong, P.P., Burkett, V.R., Codignotto, J.O., Hay, J.E., McLean, R.F., Ragoonaden, S. and Woodroffe, C.D, "*Coastal systems and low-lying areas. Climate change, impacts, adaptation and vulnerability*", in M.L. Parry, O.F. Canziani, J.P. Palutikof, P.J. van der Linden and C.E. Hanson, ed., Contribution of Working Group II to the Fourth Assessment Report of the Intergovernmental Panel on Climate Change, Cambridge University Press Cambridge, 2007, pp. 317.
17. For an excellent analysis see Dennis Rumley, "Ideology, carbon emissions and climate change discourses in the Indian Ocean Region", *Journal of the Indian Ocean Region*, vol. 2, pp.147 -154. Also see the special issue *of Journal of the Indian Ocean Region*, vol. 6, no. 2, 2010.
18. Ibid, see also Ross Garnaut, *Climate Change Review*, Commonwealth of Australia, Canberra, 2008, p.150.
19. Dennis Rumley, "Ideology, carbon emissions and climate change discourses in the Indian Ocean Region", *Journal of the Indian Ocean Region*, vol. 6, no. 2, 2010, pp. 147-154.
20. Eero Palmujoki "International Organisations and the Rhetoric of Climate Change", *Journal of the Indian Ocean Region*, vol. 6, no. 2, 2010.
21. Ian Bailey, "Neoliberalism, Climate Governance and the Scalar Politics of EU Emission Trading", *Area*, vol. 39, no. 34, p. 433.
22. *National Adaptation Program of* Action (NAPA), Ministry for the Coordination of Environmental Affairs (MICOA), Government of Mozambique. Approved by the Council of Ministers at its 32nd Session, 4 December 2007, Maputo.
23. Ibid. p. 3.
24. Ibid. p. 1.
25. Ibid. p. 42.
26. Ibid.
27. Sanjay Chaturvedi and Doyle Timothy "Geopolitics of fear and the emergence of 'climate refugees': imaginative geographies of climate change and displacements

in Bangladesh", *Journal of the Indian Ocean Region*, vol. 6, no. 2, 2010, pp. 206-222.

28. UNDP, *Reducing Disaster Risk: A Challenge for Development, Disaster Reduction Unit, Bureau for Crisis Prevention and Recovery*, John S. Swift Co, New York, 2004.
29. Ibid.
30. Nicholls, R.J., Wong, P.P., Burkett, V.R., Codignotto, J.O., Hay, J.E., McLean, R.F., Ragoonaden, S. and Woodroffe, C.D, "Coastal systems and low-lying areas. Climate change, impacts, adaptation and vulnerability", in M.L. Parry, O.F. Canziani, J.P. Palutikof, P.J. van der Linden and C.E. Hanson, ed., *Contribution of Working Group II to the Fourth Assessment Report of the Intergovernmental Panel on Climate Change*, Cambridge University Press, Cambridge, 2007, p. 337.
31. Ibid. pp. 326.
32. United Nations (2009), Address by her Excellency Sheikh Hasina Hon'ble Prime Minister, Government of the People's Republic of Bangladesh, The United Nations, New York, 26 September. Available at http://www.un.org/en/ga/64/generaldebate/pdf/BD_en.pdf, accessed on 15 November 2010.
33. Ibid.
34. Government of Bangladesh (2009), Bangladesh Climate Change Strategy an Action Plan 2009. Dhaka: Ministry of Environment and Forests, Government of the People's Republic of Bangladesh. p. xi.
35. Ibid. p. 17.
36. Sanjay Chaturvedi and Timothy Doyle, "Geopolitics of Fear and the Emergence of 'Climate Refugees': Imaginative Geographies of Climate Change and Displacements in Bangladesh", *Journal of the Indian Ocean Region*, vol. 6, no. 2, 2010, pp. 206-222.
37. Grant, H., Randerson, J. and Vidal, J. (2009), 'UK should open borders to climate refugees, says Bangladeshi minister', The Guardian, 4 December. Available at http://www.guardian. co.uk/environment/2009/nov/30/rich-west-climate-change/print, accessed 8 September 2010.
38. The Indian Sundarbans Delta is bounded by the Ichamati-Raimangal River in the east, by the Hugli River in the west, by the Bay of Bengal in the south, and the Dampier- Hodges line drawn in 1829-1830 in the north.
39. Danda, Anamitra Anurag, Gayathri Sriskanthan, Asish Ghosh, Jayanta Bandyopadhyay and Sugata Hazra, *Indian Sundarbans Delta: A Vision*, World Wide Fund for Nature-India, New Delhi, 2011, p. 7.
40. Ibid. p. 35.
41. Ibid. p. 31.
42. See Somini Sengupta, "India's River Delta Islands Washing Away", *The New York Times*, 10 April 2007; *The Hindu* (New Delhi) 24 March 2010.
43. Eva Lovbrand and Johannes Stripple, "The Climate as Political Space: On the Territorialisation of the Global Carbon Cycle", *Review of International Studies*, vol. 32, 2006, pp. 217-235.
44. Ibid. p. 217.
45. See Timothy Doyle and Sanjay Chaturvedi, "Climate Territories: A Global Soul for Global South?", *Geopolitics*, vol. 15, 2010, pp. 516-535.

46. Ibid.
47. Sugata Bose, *A Hundred Horizons: The Indian Ocean in the Age of Global Empire*, Harvard University Press, Cambridge, 2006.
48. Simon Dalby, *Security and Environmental Change*, Polity Press, Cambridge, 2009.
49. Philip E. Steinberg, *The Social Construction of the Ocean*, Cambridge University Press Cambridge, 2001.
50. Ibid.
51. Don Berlin, "Sea power, land power and the Indian Ocean", *Journal of the Indian Ocean Region,* vol. 6, no. 1, 2010, pp. 52-56.
52. Philip E, Steinberg "Navigating to Multiple Horizons: Toward a Geography of Ocean-Space", *Journal of the Professional Geographer,* vol. 51, no. 3, 1999, p. 367.
53. Nelson Mandela cited in Sugata Bose, *A Hundred Horizons: The Indian Ocean in the Age of Global Empire,* Harvard University Press, 2006, p. 281.
54. Ibid.
55. Sidney Tarrow, *The New Transnational Activism*, Cambridge University Press, Cambridge/New York, 2005.
56. I am grateful to Professor Timothy Doyle for bringing this work and the notion of embedded cosmopolitanism' to my attention.
57. Sugata Bose, *A hundred horizons: the Indian Ocean in the age of global empire,* Harvard University Press, 2006, p.281.
58. Ibid.
59. Cited in S. Murthy, *Mahatma Gandhi and Leo Tolstoy*, Long Beach: Long Beach Publications, 1987, p. 189.

Chapter 9

IOR-ARC Successes and Failures: Indonesian Perspectives

Ferdi Syamsir Ishak

Introduction

Indonesia has been actively engaged in the development of IOR-ARC since its inception. Indonesia shares the objectives of the IOR-ARC so that the organisation can bring great benefits for the people of Indonesia in particular, and the other state in this region in general. It is hoped that one day Indonesia would emerge as Chair of IOR-ARC. This desire will be realised after 2011, when Indonesia has completed its duties as Chairman of ASEAN.

Reinvigorating means reviving the IOR-ARC from the dead. Is IOR-ARC really dead? At the 10th Ministerial meeting of IOR-ARC in Sana'a Yemen in 2010[1], an Iranian delegate said that "the annual meetings such as this (CSO, COM) do not means at all, it is just a waste of time and money, very few of the meeting result that could realised". This pessimism arises because the plans have been prepared well in trial CSO, COM and sessions of the IORAG, IORBF and WGTI meetings are just programmes on paper. On most occasions, they did not materialise to the expectations of members States.

The same opinion was expressed in the sub-committee meeting in Muscat, Oman IORAG 2011.[2] On this occasion, all delegates agreed that the academics of IOR-ARC incorporated in the IORAG do not play a role in providing results of studies on the progress of cooperation of this organisation. What is perhaps needed is an overall improvement, not only the improvement of the IORAG, but also in the IORBF and WGTI, so as to restore or revive the IOR-ARC as a whole.[3]

I have been involved in the study of IOR-ARC since 2009, although research on this organisation has been conducted at Andalas University since 2003,[4] especially since the establishment of Indian Ocean Studies Centre (IOSC).[5] Despite this history of our engagement in IOR-ARC meetings, a lot of effort is needed to revive the IOR-ARC from its death. Efforts made by the ICWA in cooperation with IORG, should receive due appreciation to revive the IOR-ARC from its death would support the hopes of billions of inhabitants of the member state countries to become developed. The IOR-ARC is conscious of its responsibility to promote welfare of the people by improving standards of living and quality of life.[6]

IOR-ARC History and Indonesian Optimism

History of the IOR-ARC, starts from the history of Indian Ocean Rim Initiative (IORI). IORI then turned into IOR-ARC and was first established in Mauritius on March 1995 and formally launched on 6-7 March 1997. Currently, IOR-ARC has 18 member states.[7] The Association disseminates information on trade and investment regimes, with a view to develop the region's business community better understand the impediments to trade and investment within the region. Dialogue Partners[8] and the Observer[9] together support the IOR-ARC aims.[10]

IOR-ARC activities include support for on-going topical projects and work programmes conducted by member countries of shared interests under the umbrella of three separate working groups i.e. the Working Group on Trade and Investment (WGTI), the Indian Ocean Rim Business Forum (IORBF), and the Indian Ocean Rim Academic Group (IORAG). The Association holds a Council of Ministers (CoM) meeting once every two years.

Indonesia's optimism towards the establishment of IOR-ARC is very high, especially for "helping the region's business community". But until now the business community engaged in IORBF have not taken advantage of the existence of this organisation. Further, IORBF is only represented by a government representative and not by real businessmen.

This is one of the failures of the IOR-ARC forum. The same is the case with the IORAG forum and the academics have not given serious attention to the development of research-based projects. The sub-committee meeting for the IORAG in Muscat Oman in 2011 noted "The delegates re-emphasised that the Academic Group is an important body within the framework of the IOR-ARC. Its role as a leading and pioneering advisory think-tank seriously should be promoted by the secretariat and the member states and Dialogue Partners".[11]

IOR-ARC is not the only institution which engages in cooperation in the Indian Ocean, but before the birth of the IOR-ARC in 1990, the Indian Ocean had a variety of organisations for regional cooperation among member states. In the western Indian Ocean region: Southern African Development Community (SADC) and Common Market for Eastern and Southern Africa (COMESA) and the Arab League (AL) in Africa and the Middle East; South Asian Association For Regional Cooperation (SAARC) and Association of the South East Asian Nations (ASEAN) in Southeast Asia and Asia Pacific Economic Corporation (APEC) for Australia and New Zealand.

In the 1990s, there was no single organisation that united the two parts of the Indian Ocean territory. The first proposal to establish a Regional Block in this area came from the South African Foreign Minister Roelof Frederik "Pik" Botha, who delivered it in 1993. It was well received by India and Australia. Oman, Singapore and Kenya joined to finalise this forum. The seven countries form the core group, known by the name of The Indian Ocean Rim Initiative (IORI).

In 1995 two meetings were held. The first in Mauritius in March 1995 and the second in Perth Australia in June in the same year. The results of Mauritius meeting was a joint statement issued at the First Inter-Governmental Meeting of the Indian Ocean Rim Initiative, outlined the principles, objectives and areas of cooperation within the Indian Ocean Rim. The Joint Statement seeks:

(a) To promote consensus among IORI on the concept of cooperation in the Indian Ocean.
(b) To identify areas of cooperation.
(c) To formulate the steps taken in order to form a partnership of the Indian Ocean.

After the second meeting in 10-11 September 1996 in Mauritius, the Chairman of the Second Inter-Governmental Meeting noted that it was a milestone in further shaping the IOR-ARC as stated in the Charter of the Establishment of the IOR-ARC.[12] In 1996, Indian Ocean Rim Association for Regional Cooperation (IOR-ARC), emerged, which united the two regions of the Indian Ocean i.e. the Western Region and Eastern Region. Currently, there are 18 members countries, 7 dialogue partners and 2 observers.

Table 1

	Full members	Date of accession
1.	Australia	March 1995
2.	Bangladesh	March 1999
3.	India	March 1995
4.	Indonesia	September 1996
5.	Iran	March 1999
6.	Kenya	March 1995
7.	Madagascar	September 1996
8.	Malaysia	September 1996
9.	Mauritius	March 1995
10.	Mozambique	September 1996
11.	Oman	March 1995
12.	Singapore	March 1995
13.	South Africa	March 1995
14.	Sri Lanka	September 1996
15.	Tanzania	September 1996
16.	Thailand	March 1999
17.	United Arab Emirates	March 1999
18.	Yemen	September 1996

Source: Wikipedia 2011.

The principle objectives of the IOR-ARC is to facilitate enhanced economic cooperation between members, with a particular focus on trade and investment liberalisation. At the beginning of the IOR-ARC, a lot of hope had been superimposed, but a few others were pessimistic of its success. Feelings of pessimism is based on the sharp differences among member countries such as culture, race, religion, economic development, and strategic interests.[13] The countries vary in the size of their populations, economies, trade, and technological development and in the composition of their GDP. Countries with high per capita income usually are very excited for new project activities while states with low per capita incomes are very rarely involved. There is a need to address this gap by the developed member states of IOR-ARC.

Table 2. GDP Per Capita IOR-ARC Member State 2009

No.	Full members	GDP (USD)	World Rank
1.	United Arab Emirates	50,070	9
2.	Australia	42,279	16
3.	Singapore	36,537	22
4.	Oman	16,207	36
5.	Malaysia	7,030	66
6.	Mauritius	6,735	67
7.	South Africa	5,786	74
8.	Iran	4,540	83
9.	Thailand	3,893	95
10.	Indonesia	2,349	117
11.	Sri Lanka	2,068	121
12.	India	1,192	132
13.	Yemen	1,118	138
14.	Kenya	738	152
15.	Bangladesh	551	158
16.	Tanzania	503	162
17.	Madagascar	438	168
18.	Mozambique	428	171

Source : World Bank (2009).

In this connection, a May 1995 speech given in New Delhi, the then-Foreign Minister, Senator Gareth Evans had noted[14] "...The region is so diffuse ... it contains sovereign states ranging in size from India with over 900 million people, to Seychelles with less than 80,000 people. Economies range in size from over $ 250 billion for our two countries (India and Australia), to less than $ 400 million for the Maldives and Comoros".

Sharp differences between large and small countries have made the organisation very slow. Based on the initial hope and optimism, the IOR-ARC has not shown results yet. This is due to various problems that occurred in the Indian Ocean organisation. Although this association has been disseminating a variety of information relating to trade and investment, but the interest of member countries to take advantage of this information is still very low. So hopes to help businesses in the region to develop cooperation between them is very less if not none at all. It will be useful to keep in mind that the purpose of establishing this organisation is to disseminate information on trade and investment regimes, with a view to helping the region's business community to better understand the impediments to trade and investment within the region.

IOR-ARC Success and Failure of Indonesian Perspective

Indonesia as a member of the IOR-ARC also believes that there should be strong efforts to revive the IOR-ARC. This organisation is like suspended animation, filled with planned activities, but poor in implementation. It is inevitable that Indonesia as a country which has a free foreign policy and has conducted active cooperation with any country in the world.[15] Bilateral cooperation is strengthened by regional cooperation and Indonesia is engaged in 16 multilateral institutions. ARF, Asia-Europe Meeting (ASEM), AMED, APEC, BIMP-EAGA, CICA, CTI, European Union, FEALAC, IOR-ARC, ACD, IMT-GT, MSG, PIF, SWPD, and NAASP.

Unfortunately, IOR-ARC is not known to the Indonesian people, may be even by regional experts in Indonesia. Indonesia is closely integrated with the ASEAN and is currently the Chairman of ASEAN and ASEAN eighteenth Heads of State meting was held in Jakarta to conduct annual meeting on 7-8 May 2011.[16] This ignorance makes IOR-ARC not socialised among the people of Indonesia unlike ASEAN which everyone is familiar with. Likewise, APEC is also very well known even by the public and stakeholders in Indonesia. What about the policy of the government of Indonesia in the IOR-ARC? To answer this question, we can follow the Indonesian government's track record in the IOR-ARC activities. Although Indonesia has been a member of the IOR-ARC[17] since March 1996, but from various projects that have been designed by IORAG only two were initiated by Indonesia i.e. providing scholarships to foreign students who went to Indonesia and collaborative research conducted by Indian Ocean Studies Centre. The absence is not due lack of interest in Indonesia to IOR-ARC and Indonesia is not out of the IOR-ARC as Seychelles, but it is just that it has not been so active as India, Iran and Mauritius have been. Indonesia has always sent its delegation to the meetings of IOR-ARC, but for now

IOR-ARC is not a main priority. This can be gleaned from the Indonesia's foreign ministry website which notes that:

> "To ensure the achievement of national goals of Indonesia, Ministry of Foreign Affairs stressed on diplomatic cooperation with countries in the international world in a series of concentric circles, which consists of :
>
> 1. The first circle is the Association of Southeast Asian Nations (ASEAN) which is the main pillar of the Indonesian nation in carrying out its foreign policy.
> 2. The second concentric circle is the ASEAN+3 (Japan, China, South Korea). Beyond that, Indonesia also held intensive working relationship with the United States and the European Union which is a major economic partner of Indonesia.
> 3. The third concentric circle, Indonesia recognises the importance of it is partnering with like-minded developing countries".

What is evident is that in the foreign policy of Indonesia, IOR-ARC is not in the first circle, but in the third circle. This is natural because the biggest regional influence on Indonesia is ASEAN and ASEAN+3. This is due to many factors, especially economic and political factors. However, IOR-ARC being in the third circle does not mean that Indonesia does not value IOR-ARC and it is best demonstrated by Indonesia's track record in IOR-ARC since 2008.

Indonesia is a member of the IOR-ARC and is quite active. Since the meeting of Council of Ministers (COM) on 8 May 2008 in Tehran, Indonesia has been directly involved in several projects of the IOR-ARC such as Training on Micro-Finance, offering scholarship programme Cooperation of Developing Countries and Programme for Non-degree Dharmasiswa. In addition, Indonesia also had the opportunity to share knowledge related to strategic actions Indonesia in dealing with bird flu in Indonesia.[18]

In 2010, Indonesia participated in various activities and work programmes of the IOR-ARC, both at home and abroad. In the country, together with the Director of Intra Regional Cooperation in Asia Pacific and Africa Affairs, Ministry of Foreign Affairs (KIK ASPASAF RI) engaged in socialising IOR-ARC activities and programmes including the design of the international activities of the IOR-ARC. It is planned to hold an international a seminar by the Foreign Ministry of Indonesia in cooperation with the IORG in order to commemorate the 15th anniversary of the founding IOR-ARC. The socialisation and programme design work by KIK ASPASAF in Palembang in South Sumatra produced a book about the rise of IOR-ARC.[19] Overseas Ministry of Foreign Affairs is also very active to design and follow the events that are significant for revival IOR-ARC in Indonesia:

(a) Iran Biotech 2010, 13-15 April 2010, in Iran, Indonesia was represented by Singgih Wibowo from B2R2KP, Ministry of Maritime Affairs and Fisheries.

(b) Specialised Training Course for Foreign Diplomats for IOR-ARC Member States, 28 April–11 May 2010.

(c) Regional Experts Meeting on Herbal Medicine Processing IOR-ARC, Tehran, 19-21 May 2010, Indonesia was represented by a representative of PT. Martina Berto. As a follow up meeting will be established Indian Ocean Rim Traditional Medicine Network (IORTMNET) and India have agreed to host a similar meeting in 2012.

In addition, Indonesia also actively involved in several sub-committees that addresses specific issues such as:

(a) Member of Governing Committee for the Special Fund since the year 2008-10.

(b) Members of the Sub-Committee for discussion of restructuring the Indian Ocean Rim Academic Group (IORAG) that proposed by Oman.

(c) Members of the Sub Committee for discussion of amendments to the statutes of the University Mobility in the Indian Ocean Region (UMIOR).

The Interests of Indonesia in the Indian Ocean

Dr.Hasjim Djalal said that the Indian Ocean is the future ocean for Indonesia. The future has arrived today, so the hope is to be realised. How to make it happen is to be the initiator of this organisation, namely the Chairman of the Organisation. Assessed by Dr. Hasjim Djalal, there are 4 major interests in the Indian Ocean (a) security, (b) economic, (c) political, and (d) social and cultural interests.

Security in the Indian Ocean is currently experiencing a serious disruption. Ship-hijacking in the Indian Ocean is committed by Somali pirates and this has caused insecurity for shipping passing through the Indian Ocean.

Economic interests is a major issue in Indonesia's efforts to establish cooperation with the State in the Indian Ocean region. However, the Pacific region is more promising than in the Indian Ocean region. This is so due to the fact that there are more rich and prosperous countries in the Pacific region, while the Indian Ocean is dominated by poor countries with a low per capita income. These trends and patterns of thought must be changed by :

(a) Convincing IOR-ARC member states that the trade potential between them is very large and need to be developed jointly.
(b) States which have high per capita incomes (Australia, United Arab Emirates, Singapore and China) to strengthen trade with member countries.

Indonesia IOR-ARC Chairman Candidate

There is a discourse in Indonesia about Indonesia assuming the chairmanship of IOR-ARC after Australia. This desire will be realised after 2011, i.e. when Indonesia has completed its duties as Chairman of ASEAN and is the vice chairman at the time when Australia became chairman in 2013. The discourse has emerged in the academic world of Indonesia and has received a positive response from the government. The study shows that Indonesia has a 'lever factor' and has good relations with all member states and has the potential to strengthen the IOR-ARC in global forums. This discourse evolved has evolved in line with government policy to make Indian Ocean a prosperous and developed region. This discourse is supported by various studies and research undertaken by the Indian Ocean Studies Centre.

A statement of Deputy Minister of Foreign Affairs H.E. Triyono Wibowo at the opening of the Seminar and Workshop in Padang notes about the importance of the role of Indonesia in the Indian Ocean today signalled that Indonesia would take the role as Chairman of the IOR-ARC and Indonesia should "Utilize Cooperation of IOR-ARC for Region Interest".

Conclusions and Recommendations

(a) IOR-ARC is not dead but dormant; so that needs to be revived in many ways one of which is to empower the existing three pillars IORAG, IORBF and WGTI in an intensive coordination since they do not work on their own.

(b) IOR-ARC member states which have great economic potential should give attention to countries with limited economies so that they can develop too.

(c) Indonesia should consider the importance of IOR-ARC and work towards becoming the chairman of IOR-ARC in 2015.

END NOTES

1. Report of the 12th Meeting of the Committee of Senior Officials (CSO), IOR-ARC Secretariat, Sana'a, Republic of Yemen, 3-4 August 2010.
2. Report on the Sub-Committee Meeting of IORAG on Restructuring and Improvement of the Indian Ocean-Rim Academic Group (IORAG) Muscat, Sultanate of Oman, 12-13 February 2011.
3. The Delegates re-emphasised that the Academic Group is an Important Body within the framework of the IOR-ARC. Its role as a leading and pioneering advisory think-tank seriously should be promoted by the Secretariat and the Member States and Dialogue Partners.
4. Team Assessment and Writing Section of International Law, Faculty of Law, cooperation between the Faculty of Law University of Andalas with the Agency for the Assessment and Application of Policy (IRB) of the Department of Foreign Affairs of the Republic of Indonesia; Reinventing Diplomacy The Indian Ocean Indonesia: Efforts to Increase Role of Indonesia through the IOR-ARC, 2003-04.
5. Top initiative agency for the Assessment and Application of Policy (IRB) of the Department of Foreign Affairs of the Republic of Indonesia, 1 April 2003.
6. Preamble Charter of the Indian Ocean Rim Association for Regional Cooperation (IOR-ARC).
7. Australia, Bangladesh, India, Indonesia, Iran, Kenya, Madagascar, Malaysia, Mauritius, Mozambique, Oman, Singapore, South Africa, Sri Lanka, Tanzania, Thailand, the United Arab Emirates, and Yemen.
8. China, Egypt, France, Japan and the United Kingdom.
9. Indian Ocean Tourism Organisation (ITO) and the Indian Ocean Research Group (IORG).
10. (a) To promote the sustained growth and balanced development of the region and of the member states and to create common ground for economic cooperation region;

    (b) To focus on those areas of economic cooperation the which provide maximum opportunities to develop shared interests and mutual benefits reap. Towards this end, to formulate and implement projects for economic cooperation relating to trade facilitation, promotion and liberalisation; promotion of foreign investment, scientific and technological exchanges, and tourism, movement of natural persons and service providers on a non-discriminatory basis; and development of infrastructure and human resources, as laid down in the Work Programmes of the Association;

(c) To identify other areas of cooperation as may be mutually agreed;

(d) Towards promoting liberalisation, to remove impediments to, and lower barriers towards, freer and enhanced flow of goods, services, investment and technology within the region;

(e) To explore all possibilities and avenues for trade liberalisation with a view to augmenting and diversifying trade flows among member states;

(f) To encourage close interaction of trade and industry, academic institutions, scholars and peoples of the member states without and discrimination among member states and without prejudice to obligations under other regional economic and trade cooperation arrangements;

(g) To strengthen cooperation and dialogue among member states in international fora on global economic issues, and nowhere desirable to develop shared strategies and take common positions in the international fora on issues of mutual interest; and

(h) To promote cooperation in development of human resources, particularly through linkages among closer training institutions, universities and other specialised institutions of the member states.

11. Report on the Sub-Committee Meeting of IORAG on Restructuring and Improvement of the Indian Ocean-Rim Academic Group (IORAG) Muscat, Sultanate of Oman, 12-13 February, 2011.
    Item 6: Reform Measures Suggested by Various Member States.
12. Recalling the Joint Statement issued at the first Inter-Governmental Meeting of the Indian Ocean Rim Initiative held in Mauritius on 31 March 1995, outlining the principles, objectives and areas of cooperation within the Indian Ocean Rim; Also recalling the report of the Chairman of the Second Inter-Governmental Meeting held in Mauritius on 10-11 September 1996.
13. Indonesians Ministery of Foreign Affairs Booklet.
14. Leighton G. Luke: http://www.futuredirections.org.au/admin/uploaded_pdf.
15. Currently, Indonesia has established bilateral cooperation with 162 countries as well as a special territory in the form of non-self governing territory. Cooperation partner countries Indonesia is divided into eight regions are: Africa, Middle East, East Asia and Pacific, South Asia and Central, North and Central America, South America and the Caribbean, Western Europe, Central & Eastern Europe.
16. 18th ASEAN Summit, Jakarta Convention Center.
17. ANNEX B ALL IOR Analyis 1997-2010 AG Projects.
18. http://www.kemlu.go.id/Pages/IFPDisplay.aspx?Name=RegionalCooperation&IDP=6&P=Regional&l=id.
19. Seminar and Workshop on Role of Indonesia in the Indian Ocean Rim Organisation Association for Regional Cooperation (IOR-Arc) Post-Meeting The 10th Council Of Ministers (com) Palembang, 25-26 November 2010.

APPENDIX 1

Charter of the Indian Ocean Rim Association for Regional Cooperation (IOR-ARC)

Approved at the Tenth Meeting of the Council of Ministers, Sana'a, Republic of Yemen, 5 August 2010

PREAMBLE

The Governments of Australia, Bangladesh, India, Indonesia, Islamic Republic of Iran, Kenya, Madagascar, Malaysia, Mauritius, Mozambique, Sultanate of Oman, Singapore, South Africa, Sri Lanka, Tanzania, Thailand, United Arab Emirates and Yemen:

CONSCIOUS of historical bonds created through millennia among the peoples of the Indian Ocean Rim and with a sense of recovery of history;

COGNIZANT of economic transformation and speed of change the world over which is propelled significantly by increased intensity in regional economic co-operation;

REALISING that the countries washed by the Indian Ocean in their diversity, offer vast opportunities to enhance economic interaction and co-operation over a wide spectrum to mutual benefit and in a spirit of equality;

CONVINCED that the Indian Ocean Rim, by virtue of past shared experience and geo-economic linkages among Member States, is poised for the creation of an effective Association and practical modalities of economic co-operation; and

CONSCIOUS of their responsibility to promote the welfare of their peoples by improving their standards of living and quality of life, and having decided to revise and amend the Charter of the Indian Ocean Rim Association for Regional Co-operation (IOR-ARC) which was adopted at the first Ministerial Meeting on 5-7 March, 1997 in Mauritius;

have adopted the following:

1. Definitions

For the purpose of this Charter, the terms used in the Charter are defined as follows, unless the context otherwise indicates:

(a) "Association" means Indian Ocean Rim Association for Regional Cooperation, which may also be referred to as "IOR-ARC";
(b) "Member States" means the Member States of the IOR-ARC
(c) "Observer" means the States/Organizations which are granted Observer Status by the IOR-ARC
(d) "Dialogue Partners" means States/Organizations with which IOR-ARC enjoys consultative relationships in agreed areas of common interest.
(e) "IOR-ARC Region" means the territories of the Member States.
(f) "Council of Ministers" means the Council of Ministers (COM) of the IOR-ARC.
(g) "Committee of Senior Officials" means the Committee of Senior Officials (CSO) of the IOR-ARC.
(h) Indian Ocean Rim Academic Group (IORAG) means the Group of nominated academics from Member States
(i) Indian Ocean Rim Business Forum (IORBF) means the nominated representatives of the private sector
(j) Working Group on Trade and Investment (WGTI) means the nominated representatives from Government responsible for trade and economic cooperation.
(k) "Working Group of Heads of Mission" (WGHM) means the Ambassadors/Heads of Mission of the IOR-ARC Member States based in Pretoria, Republic of South Africa or as decided otherwise.
(l) "Specialized Agencies" means the organs of IOR-ARC established by the decision of the Member States.
(m) "Secretariat" means the Secretariat of the IOR-ARC in Mauritius,
(n) "Secretary-General" means the Secretary-General of the IOR-ARC.
(o) "Host Country/Government" means the Country/Government of the Republic of Mauritius.

2. Fundamental Principles

The Association will facilitate and promote economic, co-operation, bringing together inter-alia, representatives of Member States' governments, businesses and academia. In a spirit of multilateralism, the Association seeks to build and expand understanding and mutually beneficial co-operation through a consensus-based, evolutionary and non-intrusive approach. The Association will apply the following fundamental principles without qualification or exception to all Member States:

(a) Co-operation within the framework of the Association will be based on respect for the principles of sovereign equality, territorial integrity, political independence, non-interference in internal affairs, peaceful co-existence and mutual benefit;

(b) The membership of the Association will be open to all sovereign States of the Indian Ocean Rim which subscribe to the principles and objectives of the Charter and are willing to undertake commitments under the Charter;

(c) Decisions on all matters and issues and at all levels will be taken on the basis of consensus;

(d) Bilateral and other issues likely to generate controversy and be an impediment to regional co-operation efforts will be excluded from deliberations;

(e) Co-operation within the Association is without prejudice to rights and obligations entered into by Member States within the framework of other economic and trade co-operation arrangements which will not automatically apply to Member States of the Association. It will not be a substitute for, but seeks to reinforce, be complementary to and consistent with their bilateral, plurilateral and multilateral obligations;

(f) A member-driven approach will be followed by Member States to achieve the goals and objectives of the Association.

(g) Promotion of principles of good governance by Member States will enable smooth implementation of programmes.

3. Objectives

(a) To promote the sustained growth and balanced development of the region and of the Member States, and to create common ground for regional economic co-operation;

(b) To focus on those areas of economic co-operation which provide maximum opportunities to develop shared interests and reap mutual benefits. Towards this end, to formulate and implement projects for economic co-operation relating to trade facilitation and liberalization, promotion of foreign investment, scientific and technological exchanges, tourism, movement of natural persons and service providers on a non-discriminatory basis; and the development of infrastructure and human resources inter-alia poverty alleviation, promotion of maritime transport and related matters, cooperation in the fields of fisheries trade, research and management, aquaculture, education and training, energy, IT, health, protection of the environment, agriculture, disaster management.

(c) To explore all possibilities and avenues for trade liberalisation, to remove impediments to, and lower barriers towards, freer and enhanced flow of goods, services, investment, and technology within the region.

(d) To encourage close interaction of trade and industry, academic institutions, scholars and the peoples of the Member States without any discrimination among Member States and without prejudice to obligations under other regional economic and trade co-operation arrangements;

(e) To strengthen co-operation and dialogue among Member States in international fora on global economic issues, and where desirable to develop shared strategies and take common positions in the international fora on issues of mutual interest; and

(f) To promote co-operation in development of human resources, particularly through closer linkages among training institutions, universities and other specialised institutions of the Member States.

4. Membership

All sovereign States of the Indian Ocean Rim are eligible for membership. To become members, States must adhere to the principles and objectives enshrined in the Charter of the Association. Expansion of membership of the Association will be decided by Member States.

Council of Ministers may grant the status of Dialogue Partners or Observers to other States or Organisations, having the capacity and interest to contribute to IOR-ARC.

5. Institutional Mechanisms

(a) Council of Ministers

(i) There will be a Council of Ministers of the Association. The Council will meet annually, or more often as mutually decided, for the formulation of policies, review of progress of co-operation, decisions on new areas of co-operation, establishment of additional mechanisms and Specialized Agencies as deemed necessary, and decisions on other matters of general interest.

(ii) The Council of Ministers will elect a Chair and Vice Chair of the Association for a period of two years respectively.

(b) Committee of Senior Officials

(i) There will be a Committee of Senior Officials of the Association composed of senior government officials of Member States. It will meet annually or as often as mutually decided. It will review implementation of the decisions taken by the Council of Ministers and in cooperation with the Indian Ocean Rim Academic Group (IORAG), Indian Ocean Rim Business Forum (IORBF) and Working Group on Trade and Investment (WGTI).

(ii) The Committee of Senior Officials establishes the priorities for economic co-operation, develops, monitors and co-ordinates the Work Programmes, and mobilises resources for the financing of the Work Programmes. The Committee will submit periodic reports to the Council of Ministers, and refer as and when necessary, policy matters for the Council's decision.

(c) Indian Ocean Rim Business Forum (IORBF), Indian Ocean Rim Academic Group (IORAG) and Working Group on Trade and Investment (WGTI)

The Association includes bodies known as the Indian Ocean Rim Business Forum (IORBF), the Indian Ocean Rim Academic Group (IORAG) and Working Group on Trade and Investment (WGTI). They may meet together with the Council of Ministers and the Committee of Senior Officials or as mutually decided.

(d) Troika

(i) A"TROIKA" consisting of the Chair, the Vice Chair and the previous Chair will apply to the Council of Ministers (COM) and the Committee of Senior Officials (CSO). It will meet in the period between the meetings of the COM and CSO as often as mutually decided.

(ii) It will report to the Member States, on any important matters relating to the Association, including a review of progress, establishment of additional mechanisms, policy direction to IOR-ARC institutions, and the appointment and term of office, mandate, duties and the termination of the services of the Secretary-General.

(e) Working Group of Heads of Mission

A Working Group of Heads of Mission (WGHM), consisting of Heads of Diplomatic Mission of IOR-ARC Member States based in Pretoria, South Africa or as otherwise decided, will meet to review the periodic work programme presented by the Chair of the Council of Ministers and will act as a follow-up mechanism and should focus on issues directly referred to the WGHM by the CSO and COM.

(f) Secretariat

(i) There will be a Secretariat of the Association to manage, co-ordinate, service and monitor the implementation of policy decisions and Work Programmes, as well as prioritisation of projects as adopted by the Council of Ministers.

(ii) The Secretariat will be responsible for servicing of all IOR-ARC meetings, the representation and promotion of the Association, the collation and dissemination of information, the maintenance of an archive, depository and registry for IOR-ARC documentation and research material, and mobilization of resources.

(iii) The Secretariat will function in accordance with the provisions of the Agreement between the Government of the Republic of Mauritius and IOR-ARC relating to the rights, privileges and immunities of IOR-ARC Secretariat approved by the Council of Ministers and signed between the Government of the host country and the Secretary General.

(iv) The Secretariat will be headed by a Secretary-General who will be assisted by Directors/Experts, on voluntary secondment from Member States. In the absence of the Secretary-General, the most senior Director will act on behalf of the Secretary-General.

(v) The Secretary-General will be appointed by the Council of Ministers for a term of three years renewable for one additional term, from among candidates nominated by the Member States on the basis of qualification, experience and suitability as laid down in the staff regulations of the IOR-ARC Secretariat. He/she will be responsible to the Council of Ministers for all activities of the Association. He/she will participate in all meetings of the Council and will perform such other functions as are entrusted to him/her by these organs. He/she will provide an annual report to the Council of Ministers on the work of the Association.

(vi) The staff of the Secretariat will be appointed and governed in accordance with the terms, conditions and procedures laid down in the Staff Regulation approved by the Council of Ministers.

(g) National Focal Points

Each Member State of the Association will set up appropriate National Focal Points for IOR-ARC to co-ordinate and advance the implementation of its activities and achievement of its objectives.

(h) Specialised Agencies

Specialised agencies may be established by the decision of the Member States to promote activities in cooperation with IOR-ARC Secretariat.

6. Financial Arrangements

(a) The contribution by Member states will be determined on the basis of criteria which will be adopted by the decision of Council of Ministers.

(b) Adequate arrangements will be made by Member States financing the implementation of the Work Programmes. This will not exclude external sources of financing where appropriate.

(c) A Special Fund will be established as a financial mechanism for supporting and complementing the funding of projects and programmes adopted by the Association.

(d) The Secretariat will prepare the Budget for each year, and will submit it to Committee of Senior Officials for its consideration and recommendation for adoption by the Council of Ministers.

7. Adoption and amendment of the Charter

The (revised) Charter as well as the Rules of Procedure, Staff Regulations for the Secretariat and Financial Regulations for IOR-ARC, will take effect from the date of the adoption by the Council of Ministers.

This Charter may be amended at any time by mutual consent of Member States. Any amendments will be in writing will require the approval the Council of Ministers.

This Charter will replace the 1997 Charter of IOR-ARC

APPENDIX 2

Sana'a Communiqué 2010

On the occasion of the 10th Council of Ministers of IOR-ARC Sana'a, Republic of Yemen, 5 August 2010

The Honourable Ministers and high-ranking Officials participating in the 10th Meeting of the Council of Ministers of IOR-ARC held in Sana'a on 5th August 2010, expressed their appreciation to the Republic of Yemen, for the capable leadership given by Yemen during its second year Chairmanship of the Council of Ministers Meeting.

They noted the progress, achievements and challenges of the Association over the past year. They also welcomed the adoption of the revised Charter of IOR-ARC, Rules of Procedure, Staff Regulations and Financial Regulations which will enhance the effectiveness of the Association.

The Honourable Ministers especially emphasized the following areas:

- Implementation of the spirit of the revised Charter of IOR-ARC for revitalizing the association.
- Enhancing Member State-driven cooperation in various areas including, inter-alia the promotion of trade and investment, tourism, cultural cooperation and education.
- Full support of Member States to the operationalisation of the Fisheries Support Unit (FSU).
- Implementation of the Action Plan, adopted in the Ministerial Meeting in 2008.
- Cooperation in combating communicable diseases and natural disasters.
- Cooperation among Member States in addressing the challenges emanating from climate change.
- Encouraging Member States to actively cooperate in the different programmes of Regional Centre for Science and Transfer of Technology.

- Support for establishment of other Centres of Excellence.
- Project-driven and research-oriented initiatives to be actively carried forward and particularly to be decided and followed up by regular meetings of the CSO and between the annual meetings of the COM, entailing greater coordination amongst Member States as well as between Member States and the Secretariat.
- Commitment to the functioning of the IOR-ARC Maritime Transport Council and the promotion of maritime related issues in the Indian Ocean.
- Support initiatives for combating Piracy in the Gulf of Aden and other parts of the Indian Ocean, and support the initiative of Republic of Yemen.
- Enhancement of private sector involvement in the Association in the area of business, trade and economic cooperation with the support of leading Chambers of Commerce of each Member State for participation in the activities of IOR-ARC Business Forum.
- Greater support to the activities of the IOR-ARC Academic Group by the broader participation of leading academics, scientists and educators from each Member State.

The Government of Yemen expressed its heartfelt thanks for the support and cooperation that was offered to it by IOR-ARC Member States during its tenure as Chair of the Association. The delegates of Member States expressed their thanks to His Excellency, Ali Abdullah Saleh, President of Republic of Yemen for his support of the Association activities, and the Prime Minister of Republic of Yemen for his Opening Ceremony Speech. The delegates of Member States expressed their gratefulness and appreciation for hospitality offered to them by the Government and people of Yemen and for the excellent organization of the Meeting.

APPENDIX 3

Sana'a Communiqué 2009

On the occasion of the 9th Council of Ministers of IOR-ARC Sana'a, Republic of Yemen, 25 June 2009

The Ministers and Heads of Delegations participating in the 9th Council of Ministers Meeting of IOR-ARC in Sana'a during the period 20–25th of June 2009 expressed their appreciation for the warm hospitality extended by the Republic of Yemen and the excellent arrangements for the IOR-ARC meetings. Member States also expressed their support for the development and prosperity of Yemen and its people.

The Council of Ministers noted the active participation of Member States in all meetings of IOR-ARC, which reflects their commitment to the Association's role in enhancing greater cooperation between Member States in the field of trade, investment, academic exchanges and technical cooperation.

The Council of Ministers also stressed the importance of support to the Secretariat so as to enable it to execute its responsibilities in an efficient and dynamic manner.

The Council of Ministers approved the following activities:

1. The Re-examination of the Charter to better address the changing needs of the Association.
2. Encourage Member States to be represented by technical experts in the meetings of the technical fora.
3. Appoint a review panel to prioritize and review the projects submitted to the different fora of IOR-ARC
4. Abandon any projects which did not show any progress during the last two years after consultation with the lead coordinator Member State.

The Council of Ministers supported projects for the establishment of the Regional Centre for Science and Technology Transfer, the

Maritime Transport Council, the Fisheries Support Unit and the Preferential Trade Arrangement for the mutual benefit of participating Member States.

The Council of Ministers encouraged expanding the cooperation between IOR-ARC Member States in various areas including Investment, Tourism, Construction, Trade, Education and Training, Protection of the Environment and New Renewable Energy, Agro-metrological advisory service system to increase agricultural output and forecasting the track, intensity, landfall prediction and impact assessment of tropical cyclones affecting the north Indian Ocean Rim Countries etc.

IOR-ARC Member States expressed their full support to the Yemen initiative and its efforts to combat piracy as well as the efforts of other countries. They welcome the idea of the concept paper to establish the Regional Maritime Centre for sharing of information for combating piracy in Yemen.

IOR-ARC Member States strongly welcomed the initiative of the United Arab Emirates to propose the hosting of the IRENA headquarters. This is in the context of ongoing global discussion on climate change where the crucial role of renewable energy resources was emphasized by all IOR-ARC Member countries.

APPENDIX 4

Tehran Communiqué 2008

On the occasion of the 8th Council of Ministers of IOR-ARC Tehran, Iran, May 4, 2008

The Honourable Ministers and high-ranking Officials participating in the 8th Council of Ministers Meeting of IOR-ARC held in Tehran on 4th May 2008, expressed their appreciation for the two consecutive tenure of Chairmanship extended by the Islamic Republic of Iran, and noted the progress, achievements and shortcomings of the Association during the past eleven years, expressed the need for further progress in advancing the objectives of the Association in the following areas:

1. The re-examination and amendment to the Charter of IOR-ARC; especially the fundamental principles related to decision making (consensus), called for undertaking structural reforms of the Association in order to make it move forward and action-oriented.
2. Due to the large scale of illegal, unregulated and unreported fishing activities, it is necessary to examine regional regulations to combat the over-fishing of migratory species (Tuna) in the Indian Ocean Rim, and for such purpose to examine the establishment of Regional Fisheries Agreements.
3. To enhance the cooperation between IOR Member States in various areas including the area of Education and Training, support Exchange Students Programs through University Mobility of Indian Ocean Rim (Region) – (UMIOR), and appreciate and support various training programmes and scholarships provided by several IOR Member States.
4. Call upon the Implementation of an Action Plan and the need to prepare a Ten Year Road Map for the future direction of the Association.
5. The need for capacity development building among Member States.

6. Encourage Member States to cooperate in the area of establishing Centres of Excellence.
7. Expedite a Fast Track mechanism to enhance private sector involvement in the Association activities in the area of Business, Trade and Economic Cooperation.
8. Protection of the environment of the Indian Ocean and its unique eco-system and species.
9. Enhancing cooperation on fossil, new and renewable energy.
10. Establishing a sustainable tourism arrangement among Member States.
11. Promoting cultural cooperation among Member States.
12. Preparing the ground for a Summit of Heads of the States to be held in mid-term.
13. Enhanced Cooperation in the priority areas.
14. Project-driven and research oriented initiatives to be actively carried forward.
15. Strengthening the Secretariat, including its financial capacity, structure, salary and allowances of personnel of the Secretariat to make it efficient and dynamic.

Index